Hope in the Dark

Untold Histories, Wild Possibilities

REBECCA SOLNIT

WITH A NEW FOREWORD AND AFTERWORD

"Rebecca Solnit is a national literary treasure: a passionate, close-to-the-ground reporter with the soul and voice of a philosopher-poet. And, unlike so many who write about the great injustices of this world, she is an optimist whose faith is deeply grounded in a knowledge of history. This is a book to give you not just hope but zest for the battles ahead."

—ADAM HOCHSCHILD

"I've found no more lucid and luminous a defense of hope than the one Rebecca Solnit launches in *Hope in the Dark*—a slim, potent book penned in the wake of the Bush administration's invasion of Iraq, a book that has grown only more relevant and poignant in the decade since."

—MARIA POPOVA

Praise for *Hope in the Dark*

"This is the ultimate 'feel-good' book for exhausted campaigners and activists . . . an intensely personal account, a meditation on activism and hope."

—*Guardian*

"Time and again she comes running towards you with a bunch of hopes she has found and picked in the undergrowth of the times we are living in. And you remember that hope is not a guarantee for tomorrow but a detonator of energy for action today."

— John Berger, author, *Ways of Seeing*

"No writer has better understood the mix of fear and possibility, peril, and exuberance that's marked this new millennium. Rebecca Solnit writes as independently as Orwell; she's a great muralist, a Diego Rivera of words. Literary and progressive America is in a Solnit moment, which, given her endless talent, should last a very long time."

— Bill McKibben, author, *Deep Economy*

"*Hope in the Dark* changed my life. During a period of pervasive cynicism and political despair, the first edition of this book provided me with a model for activist engagement that I have held dear ever since. Today, as movements for climate, racial, and economic justice sweep the globe, its message is more relevant than ever. In her inimitable and inspiring way, Solnit reminds us that social change follows an unpredictable path. Despite all the obstacles, we must not lose sight of the fact profound transformation is possible. This book's compact size belies its true power. It provides succor and sustenance, fuel and fire for those fighting for a more just world."

—Astra Taylor, author, *The People's Platform*

"Rebecca Solnit is a national literary treasure: a passionate, close-to-the-ground reporter with the soul and voice of a philosopher-poet. And, unlike so many who write about the great injustices of this world, she is an optimist whose faith is deeply grounded in a knowledge of history. This is a book to give you not just hope but zest for the battles ahead."

— **Adam Hochschild, author,** *King Leopold's Ghost*

Praise for earlier editions

"In this inspired meditation on the very nature of action and the reasons one thing leads to another, Rebecca Solnit, with her customary intellectual penetration, freshness of expression, and high elegance, finds new springs of hope in dark times."

— **Jonathan Schell**

"Seemingly lost in the woods of deceit and banality, bereft of hope, we are confronted by Rebecca Solnit and her astonishing flashlight. In a jewel of a book that is poetic in substance as well as style, she reveals where we were, where we are, and the step-by-step advances that have been made in human rights, as we stubbornly stumble out of the darkness."

— **Studs Terkel**

"In this extraordinary book, Rebecca Solnit's prose grows poetic wings that enable her to soar to a visionary height. The good news that she brings back is that our struggles—with persistence and courage—are indeed the seeds of kindness."

— **Mike Davis**

"Can you imagine a cross between Joan Rivers and Simone de Beauvoir? I didn't think so, but no likelier hybrid comes to mind... Solnit is the real activist deal: the type who gets arrested at nuclear test sites and mans the barricades at the World Trade Organization demonstrations in Seattle. She's also the real freelance intellectual deal: the much rarer type who earns her living generating reams of thoughtful, wide-ranging nonfiction."

—Newsday

"An inspired observer and passionate historian, [Solnit] is one of the most creative, penetrating, and eloquent cultural critics writing today. In her most personal critique to date, she reflects on the crucial, often underrated accomplishments of grassroots activists. Solnit contemplates such well-studied revolutions as the American civil rights movement and the fall of the Berlin Wall, but more significantly she reflects on such recent events as successful protests against nuclear testing in Nevada, the Zapatista uprising, the anti-corporate globalization movement, the "unprecedented global wave of protest" against the war in Iraq, and such hopeful ecological successes as the return of wolves to Yellowstone and the restoration of the Los Angeles River. Solnit's rousing celebration of people who work tirelessly behind the scenes and courageously on the streets for justice and environmental health harmonizes beautifully with Studs Terkel's *Hope Dies Last*, and helps readers understand more clearly where we stand as individuals, as Americans, and as citizens of the world."

— Donna Seaman, *Booklist*

"This slim volume, to quote the author's own reflections on the quincentennial of Columbus's discovery of America, is 'a zigzag trail of encounters, reactions, and realizations.' Solnit, recent winner of an NBCC award for criticism for *River of Shadows: Eadweard Muybridge and the Technological Wild West*, rambles from place to place and topic to topic in a discursive examination of the current state of leftist protest and activism. Unwilling to accept the bleak, almost apocalyptic worldview of many of her progressive counterparts, Solnit celebrates the hope and optimism that recent episodes reveal. She points to the resurrection of indigenous causes represented by Zapatismo, the WTO protests in Seattle and Cancun, and the worldwide protests against the US-led war in Iraq, and other smaller, more marginal protests. Solnit argues persuasively that engaged, thoughtful dissent is far healthier today than many believe. Activists, who operate by nature on the fringes of hierarchies of economy and power, often fail to recognize the power of activity that seems inconsequential. Her goal, in essence, is 'to throw out the crippling assumptions with which many activists proceed.'"

—Publishers Weekly

Hope in the Dark

Untold Histories,
Wild Possibilities

Third Edition
with a new foreword and afterword

Rebecca Solnit

Haymarket Books
Chicago, Illinois

First published in the United States by Nation Books in 2004
© Rebecca Solnit 2016

Published in 2016 by
Haymarket Books
P.O. Box 180165
Chicago, IL 60618
773-583-7884
www.haymarketbooks.org
info@haymarketbooks.org

ISBN: 978-1-60846-576-7

Trade distribution:
In the US, Consortium Book Sales and Distribution, www.cbsd.com
In Canada, Publishers Group Canada, www.pgcbooks.ca
In the UK, Turnaround Publisher Services, www.turnaround-uk.com
All other countries, Publishers Group Worldwide, www.pgw.com

This book was published with the generous support of Lannan
Foundation and Wallace Action Fund.

Cover design by Abby Weintraub.

Printed in Canada by union labor.

Library of Congress Cataloging-in-Publication data is available.

10 9 8 7 6

Contents

Nothing that has ever happened should be regarded as lost for history.
—Walter Benjamin

If you don't like the news . . . go out and make some of your own.
—Newsman Wes Nisker's closing salutation
on radio station KSAN in the 1970s

Foreword to the Third Edition (2015)

Grounds for Hope

Your opponents would love you to believe that it's hopeless, that you have no power, that there's no reason to act, that you can't win. Hope is a gift you don't have to surrender, a power you don't have to throw away. And though hope can be an act of defiance, defiance isn't enough reason to hope. But there are good reasons.

I wrote this book in 2003 and early 2004 to make the case for hope. The text that follows is in some ways of its moment—it was written against the tremendous despair at the height of the Bush administration's powers and the outset of the war in Iraq. That moment passed long ago, but despair, defeatism, cynicism, and the amnesia and assumptions from which they often arise have not dispersed, even as the most wildly, unimaginably magnificent things came to pass. There is a lot of evidence for the defense.

Coming back to the text more than a dozen tumultuous years later, I believe its premises hold up. Progressive, populist, and grassroots constituencies have had many victories. Popular power has continued to be a profound force for change. And the changes we've undergone, both wonderful and terrible, are astonishing. The world of 2003 has been swept away. Its damage lingers, but its arrangements and many of its ideologies have given way to new ones—and, more than that, to a sea change in who we are and how we imagine ourselves, the world, and so many things in it.

This is an extraordinary time full of vital, transformative movements that could not be foreseen. It's also a nightmarish time. Full engagement requires the ability to perceive both. The twenty-first century has seen the rise of hideous economic inequality, perhaps due to amnesia both of the working people who countenance declines in wages, working conditions, and social services, and the elites who forgot that they conceded to some of these things in the hope of avoiding revolution. The rise of Silicon Valley as a global power center has eliminated and automated countless jobs, enhancing economic inequality; it has produced new elites and monstrous corporations from Amazon, with its attack on publishing, authors, and working conditions, to Google, which is attempting to build a global information monopoly in myriad arenas and in the process amassing terrifying powers, including the power that comes with sophisticated profiles of most computer users. The major tech companies have created and deployed surveillance capacities that the Kremlin and FBI at the height of the Cold War could not have dreamed of—in collaboration with the government that should be regulating them. The attack on civil liberties, including the right to privacy, continues long after its Global War on Terror justifications have faded away.

Worse than these is the arrival of climate change, faster, harder, and more devastating than scientists anticipated.

Hope doesn't mean denying these realities. It means facing them and addressing them by remembering what else the twenty-first century has brought, including the movements, heroes, and shifts in consciousness that address these things now. Among them: Occupy Wall Street; Black Lives Matter; Idle No More; the Dreamers addressing the Dream Act and immigration rights; Edward Snowden, Laura Poitras, Glenn Greenwald, and the movement for corporate and government transparency; the push for marriage equality; a resurgent feminist movement; economic justice movements addressing (and in many cases raising) minimum wage and fighting debt peonage and the student-loan racket; and a dynamic climate and climate justice movement—and the intersections between them all. This has been a truly remarkable decade for movement-building, social change, and deep, profound shifts in ideas, perspective, and frameworks for broad parts of the population (and, of course, backlashes against all those things).

The Uses of Uncertainty

Hope in the Dark began as an essay that I published online about six weeks after the United States launched its war on Iraq. It immediately went, as they say, viral—it was widely circulated by email, picked up by a mainstream newspaper and many news websites, pirated by some alternative newspapers, even printed out and distributed by hand by someone who liked it. It was my first adventure in online publishing, as well as in speaking directly to the inner life of the politics of the moment, to the emotions and perceptions that underlie our political positions and engagements. Amazed by the ravenous appetite for another way of telling who and where we were, I decided to write this slender book. It has had an interesting life in several languages, and it's a pleasure to revise it with this introduction and a few new chapters at the end, notes, and handsome redesign. Updating the book would have meant writing an entirely new book, so we chose to reissue the 2005 second edition with this additional material instead.

After the book was published, I spent years on the road talking about hope and activism, the historical record and the possibilities, and my arguments grew, perhaps, more polished or more precise or at least more case-hardened. Here's another traverse across that landscape.

It's important to say what hope is not: it is not the belief that everything was, is, or will be fine. The evidence is all around us of tremendous suffering and tremendous destruction. The hope I'm interested in is about broad perspectives with specific possibilities, ones that invite or demand that we act. It's also not a sunny everything-is-getting-better narrative, though it may be a counter to the everything-is-getting-worse narrative. You could call it an account of complexities and uncertainties, with openings. "Critical thinking without hope is cynicism, but hope without critical thinking is naïvete," the Bulgarian writer Maria Popova recently remarked. And Patrisse Cullors, one of the founders of Black Lives Matter, early on described the movement's mission as to "Provide hope and inspiration for collective action to build collective power to achieve collective transformation, rooted in grief and rage but pointed towards vision and dreams." It's a statement that acknowledges that grief and hope can coexist.

The tremendous human rights achievements—not only in gaining rights but in redefining race, gender, sexuality, embodiment, spiritual-ity, and the idea of the good life—of the past half century have flow-ered during a time of unprecedented ecological destruction and the rise of innovative new means of exploitation. And the rise of new forms of resistance, including resistance enabled by an elegant understanding of that ecology and new ways for people to communicate and organize, and new and exhilarating alliances across distance and difference.

Hope locates itself in the premises that we don't know what will happen and that in the spaciousness of uncertainty is room to act. When you recognize uncertainty, you recognize that you may be able to influence the outcomes—you alone or you in concert with a few dozen or several million others. Hope is an embrace of the unknown and the unknowable, an alternative to the certainty of both optimists and pessimists. Optimists think it will all be fine without our involve-ment; pessimists take the opposite position; both excuse themselves from acting. It's the belief that what we do matters even though how and when it may matter, who and what it may impact, are not things we can know beforehand. We may not, in fact, know them afterward either, but they matter all the same, and history is full of people whose influence was most powerful after they were gone.

There are major movements that failed to achieve their goals; there are also comparatively small gestures that mushroomed into successful revolutions. The self-immolation of impoverished, police-harassed produce-seller Mohamed Bouazizi on December 17, 2010, in Tunisia was the spark that lit a revolution in his country and then across northern Africa and other parts of the Arab world in 2011. And though the civil war in Syria and the counterrevolutions after Egypt's extraordinary uprising might be what most remember, Tunisia's "jasmine revolution" toppled a dictator and led to peaceful elections in that country in 2014. Whatever else the Arab Spring was, it's an extraordinary example of how unpredictable change is and how potent popular power can be. And five years on, it's too soon to draw conclusions about what it all meant.

You can tell the genesis story of the Arab Spring other ways. The quiet organizing going on in the shadows beforehand matters. So does the comic book about Martin Luther King and civil disobedience that was translated into Arabic and widely distributed in Egypt shortly before the Arab Spring. You can tell of King's civil disobedience tactics being inspired by Gandhi's tactics, and Gandhi's inspired by Tolstoy and the radical acts of noncooperation and sabotage of British women suffragists. So the threads of ideas weave around the world and through the decades and centuries. There's another lineage for the Arab Spring in hip-hop, the African American music that's become a global medium for dissent and outrage; Tunisian hip-hop artist El Général was, along with Bouazizi, an instigator of the uprising, and other musicians played roles in articulating the outrage and inspiring the crowds.

Mushroomed: after a rain mushrooms appear on the surface of the earth as if from nowhere. Many do so from a sometimes vast underground fungus that remains invisible and largely unknown. What we call mushrooms mycologists call the fruiting body of the larger, less visible fungus. Uprisings and revolutions are often considered to be spontaneous, but less visible long-term organizing and groundwork— or underground work—often laid the foundation. Changes in ideas and values also result from work done by writers, scholars, public intellectuals, social activists, and participants in social media. It seems insignificant or peripheral until very different outcomes emerge from transformed assumptions about who and what matters, who should be heard and believed, who has rights.

Ideas at first considered outrageous or ridiculous or extreme gradually become what people think they've always believed. How the transformation happened is rarely remembered, in part because it's compromising: it recalls the mainstream when the mainstream was, say, rabidly homophobic or racist in a way it no longer is; and it recalls that power comes from the shadows and the margins, that our hope is in the dark around the edges, not the limelight of center stage. Our hope and often our power.

The Stories We Tell

Changing the story isn't enough in itself, but it has often been foundational to real changes. Making an injury visible and public is often the first step in remedying it, and political change often follows culture, as what was long tolerated is seen to be intolerable, or what was overlooked becomes obvious. Which means that every conflict is in part a battle over the story we tell, or who tells and who is heard.

A victory doesn't mean that everything is now going to be nice forever and we can therefore all go lounge around until the end of time. Some activists are afraid that if we acknowledge victory, people will give up the struggle. I've long been more afraid that people will give up and go home or never get started in the first place if they think no victory is possible or fail to recognize the victories already achieved. Marriage equality is not the end of homophobia, but it's something to celebrate. A victory is a milestone on the road, evidence that sometimes we win, and encouragement to keep going, not to stop. Or it should be.

My own inquiry into the grounds for hope has received two great reinforcements since I wrote *Hope in the Dark*. One came from the recognition of how powerful are the altruistic, idealistic forces already at work in the world. Most of us would say, if asked, that we live in a capitalist

society, but vast amounts of how we live our everyday lives—our inter-
actions with and commitments to family lives, friendships, avocations,
membership in social, spiritual, and political organizations—are in essence noncapitalist or even anticapitalist, full of things we do for free, out
of love, and on principle.

In a way, capitalism is an ongoing disaster anticapitalism allevi-
ates, like a mother cleaning up after her child's messes (or, to extend
the analogy, sometimes disciplining that child to clean up after itself,
through legislation or protest, or preventing some of the messes in
the first place, and it might be worth adding that noncapitalist ways
of doing things are much older than free-market economic arrangements). Activists often speak as though the solutions we need have not
yet been launched or invented, as though we are starting from scratch,
when often the real goal is to amplify the power and reach of existing
alternatives. What we dream of is already present in the world.

The second reinforcement came out of my investigation of how
human beings respond to major urban disasters, from the devastating
earthquakes in San Francisco (in 1906) and Mexico City (in 1985) to
the Blitz in London to Hurricane Katrina in New Orleans. The assumption behind much disaster response by the authorities—and the logic of
bombing civilians—is that civilization is a brittle façade, and behind it
lies our true nature as monstrous, selfish, chaotic, and violent or as tim-
id, fragile, and helpless. In fact, in most disasters most people are calm,
resourceful, altruistic, and creative. And civilian bombing campaigns
generally fail to break the will of the people, making them a waste as
well as a crime against humanity.

What startled me about the response to disaster was not the virtue,
since virtue is often the result of diligence and dutifulness, but the
passionate joy that shined out from accounts by people who had barely
survived. These people who had lost everything, who were living in
rubble or ruins, had found agency, meaning, community, immediacy
in their work together with other survivors. The century of testimo-

ny I drew from for my 2009 book *A Paradise Built in Hell* suggested how much we want lives of meaningful engagement, of membership in civil society, and how much societal effort goes into withering us away from these fullest, most powerful selves. But people return to those selves, those ways of self-organizing, as if by instinct when the situation demands it. Thus a disaster is a lot like a revolution when it comes to disruption and improvisation, to new roles and an unnerving or exhilarating sense that now anything is possible.

This was a revolutionary vision of human nature and a revelation that we can pursue our ideals not out of diligence but because when they are realized there's joy, and joy is itself an insurrectionary force against the dreariness and dullness and isolation of everyday life. My own research was, I realized by its end, a small part of an enormous project going on among many disciplines—psychology, economics, neurobiology, sociology, anthropology, political science—to redefine human nature as something more communal, cooperative, and compassionate. This rescue of our reputations from the social darwinists and the Hobbesians is important, not to feel positive about ourselves but to recognize the radical possibilities that can be built on an alternative view of human nature.

The fruits of these inquiries made me more hopeful. But it's important to emphasize that hope is only a beginning; it's not a substitute for action, only a basis for it. "Not everything that is faced can be changed, but nothing can be changed until it is faced," said James Baldwin. Hope gets you there; work gets you through. "The future belongs to those who prepare for it today," said Malcolm X. And there is a long history of that work, the work to change the world, a long history of methods, heroes, visionaries, heroines, victories—and, of course, failures. But the victories matter, and remembering them matters too. "We must accept finite disappointment, but never lose infinite hope," said Martin Luther King Jr.

The Branches Are Hope; the Roots Are Memory

"Memory produces hope in the same way that amnesia produces despair," the theologian Walter Brueggeman noted. It's an extraordinary statement, one that reminds us that though hope is about the future, grounds for hope lie in the records and recollections of the past. We can tell of a past that was nothing but defeats and cruelties and injustices, or of a past that was some lovely golden age now irretrievably lost, or we can tell a more complicated and accurate story, one that has room for the best and worst, for atrocities and liberations, for grief and jubilation. A memory commensurate to the complexity of the past and the whole cast of participants, a memory that includes our power, produces that forward-directed energy called hope.

Amnesia leads to despair in many ways. The status quo would like you to believe it is immutable, inevitable, and invulnerable, and lack of memory of a dynamically changing world reinforces this view. In other words, when you don't know how much things have changed, you don't see that they are changing or that they can change. Those who think that way don't remember raids on gay bars when being queer was illegal or rivers that caught fire when unregulated pollution peaked in the 1960s or that there were, worldwide, 70 percent more seabirds a few decades ago and, before the economic shifts of the Reagan Revolution, very, very few homeless people in the United States. Thus, they don't recognize the forces of change at work.

One of the essential aspects of depression is the sense that you will always be mired in this misery, that nothing can or will change. It's what makes suicide so seductive as the only visible exit from the prison of the present. There's a public equivalent to private depression, a sense that the nation or the society rather than the individual is stuck. Things don't always change for the better, but they change, and we can play a role in that change if we act. Which is where hope comes in, and memory, the collective memory we call history.

The other affliction amnesia brings is a lack of examples of positive change, of popular power, evidence that we can do it and have done it. George Orwell wrote, "Who controls the past controls the future. Who controls the present controls the past." Controlling the past begins by knowing it; the stories we tell about who we were and what we did shape what we can and will do. Despair is also often premature: it's a form of impatience as well as of certainty.

My favorite comment about political change comes from Zhou En-Lai, a high-ranking member of Chairman Mao's government. Asked, in the early 1970s, about his opinion of the French Revolution, he answered, "Too soon to tell." Some argue that he was talking about the insurrections of 1968, not the monarchy-toppling of 1789, but even then it demonstrates a generous and expansive perspective. To retain a sense that even four years later the verdict isn't in is to live with more open-minded uncertainty than most people now can tolerate.

News cycles tend to suggest that change happens in small, sudden bursts or not at all. As I write, the military men who probably murdered Chilean singer and political activist Victor Jara in 1973 are being charged. More than forty years have gone by; some stories take far longer than that to finish. The struggle to get women the vote took nearly three-quarters of a century. For a time people liked to announce that feminism had failed, as though the project of overturning millennia of social arrangements should achieve its final victories in a few decades, or as though it had stopped. Feminism is just starting, and its manifestations matter in rural Himalayan villages, not just first-world cities. Susan Griffin, a great writer in the present who was also an important part of 1970s feminism, recently remarked, "I've seen enough change in my lifetime to know that despair is not only self-defeating, it is unrealistic."

Other changes result in victories and are then forgotten. For decades, radicals were preoccupied with East Timor, brutally occupied by Indonesia from 1975 to 2002; the liberated country is no longer news. It won its liberty because of valiant struggle from within, but also because of dedicated groups on the outside who pressured and shamed the governments supporting the Indonesian regime. We could learn quite a lot from the remarkable display of power and solidarity and East Timor's eventual victory, but the whole struggle seems forgotten.

For decades, Peabody Western Coal Corporation mined coal on the Hopi/Navajo land at Black Mesa in ways that contaminated the air and drained vast amounts of water from the region. The fight against Black Mesa was a totemic struggle for indigenous sovereignty and environmental justice; in 2005, the mines were shut down, and the issue disappeared from the conversation. It was also a case of tenacious activism from within and good allies from without, prolonged lawsuits, and perseverance.

We need litanies or recitations or monuments to these victories, so that they are landmarks in everyone's mind. More broadly, shifts in, say, the status of women are easily overlooked by people who don't remember that, a few decades ago, reproductive rights were not yet a concept, and there was no recourse for exclusion, discrimination, workplace sexual harassment, most forms of rape, and other crimes against women the legal system did not recognize or even countenanced. None of the changes were inevitable, either—people fought for them and won them.

People adjust without assessing the changes. As of 2014, Iowa gets 28 percent of its electricity from wind alone, not because someone in that conservative state declared death to all fossil fuel corporations or overthrew anyone or anything, but because it was a sensible and affordable option. Denmark, in the summer of 2015, achieved 140 percent of its electricity needs through wind generation (and sold the surplus to neighboring countries). Scotland has achieved renewable energy generation of 50 percent and set a goal of 100 percent by 2020. Thirty percent more solar was installed in 2014 than the year before in the United States, and renewables are becoming more affordable worldwide—in some places they are already cheaper than fossil-fueled energy. These incremental changes have happened quietly, and many people don't know they have begun, let alone exploded.

If there is one thing we can draw from where we are now and where we were then, it is that the unimaginable is ordinary, that the way forward is almost never a straight line you can glance down but a convoluted path of surprises, gifts, and afflictions you prepare for by accepting your blind spots as well as your intuitions. Howard Zinn wrote in 1988, in what now seems like a lost world before so many political upheavals and technological changes arrived, "As this century draws to a close, a century packed with history, what leaps out from that history is its utter unpredictability." He was, back then, wondering at the distance we'd traveled from when the Democratic National Party Convention refused to seat Blacks from Mississippi to when Jesse Jackson ran (a largely symbolic campaign) for president at a time most people thought they would never live to see a Black family occupy the White House. In that essay, "The Optimism of Uncertainty," Zinn continues,

> The struggle for justice should never be abandoned because of the apparent overwhelming power of those who have the guns and the money and who seem invisible in their determination to hold onto it. That apparent power has, again and again, proved vulnerable to moral fervor, determination, unity, organization, sacrifice, wit, ingenuity, courage, patience—whether by blacks in Alabama and South Africa, peasants in El Salvador, Nicaragua, and Vietnam, or workers and intellectuals in Poland, Hungary, and the Soviet Union itself.

People Have the Power

Social, cultural, or political change does not work in predictable ways or on predictable schedules. The month before the Berlin Wall fell, almost no one anticipated that the Soviet Bloc was going to disintegrate all of a sudden (thanks to many factors, including the tremendous power of civil society, nonviolent direct action, and hopeful organizing going back to the 1970s), any more than anyone, even the participants, foresaw the impact that the Arab Spring or Occupy Wall Street or a host of other great uprisings would have. We don't know what is going to happen, or how, or when, and that very uncertainty is the space of hope.

Those who doubt that these moments matter should note how terrified the authorities and elites are when they erupt. That fear signifies their recognition that popular power is real enough to overturn regimes and rewrite the social contract. And it often has. Sometimes your enemies know what your friends can't believe. Those who dismiss these moments because of their imperfections, limitations, or incompleteness need to look harder at what joy and hope shine out of them and what real changes have emerged because of them, even if not always in the most obvious or recognizable ways.

And everything is flawed, if you want to look at it that way. The analogy that has helped me most is this: in Hurricane Katrina, hundreds of boat-owners rescued people—single moms, toddlers, grandfathers—stranded in attics, on roofs, in flooded housing projects, hospitals, and school buildings. None of them said, *I can't rescue everyone, therefore it's futile; therefore my efforts are flawed and worthless*, though that's often what people say about more abstract issues in which, nevertheless, lives, places, cultures, species, rights are at stake. They went out there in fishing boats and rowboats and pirogues and all kinds of small craft, some driving from as far as Texas and eluding the authorities to get in, others refugees themselves working within the city. There was bumper-to-bumper boat-trailer traffic—the celebrated Cajun Navy—going *toward* the city the day after the levees broke. None of those people said, *I can't rescue them all*. All of them said, *I can rescue someone, and that's work so meaningful and important I will risk my life and defy the authorities to do it*. And they did. Of course, working for systemic change also matters—the kind of change that might prevent calamities by addressing the climate or the infrastructure or the environmental and economic injustice that put some people in harm's way in New Orleans in the first place.

Change is rarely straightforward, and that is one of the central premises of this book. Sometimes it's as complex as chaos theory and as slow as evolution. Even things that seem to happen suddenly arise from deep roots in the past or from long-dormant seeds. A young man's suicide triggers an uprising that inspires other uprisings, but the incident was a spark; the bonfire it lit was laid by activist networks and ideas about civil disobedience and by the deep desire for justice and freedom that exists everywhere.

It's important to ask not only what those moments produced in the long run but what they were in their heyday. If people find themselves living in a world in which some hopes are realized and some joys are incandescent and some boundaries between individuals and groups are lowered, even for an hour or a day or several months, that matters. Memory of joy and liberation can become a navigational tool, an identity, a gift.

Paul Goodman famously wrote, "Suppose you had the revolution you are talking and dreaming about. Suppose your side had won, and you had the kind of society that you wanted. How would you live, you personally, in that society? Start living that way now!" It's an argument for tiny and temporary victories, and for the possibility of partial victories in the absence or even the impossibility of total victories. Total victory has always seemed like a secular equivalent of paradise: a place where all the problems are solved and there's nothing to do, a fairly boring place. The absolutists of the old left imagined that victory would, when it came, be total and permanent, which is practically the same as saying that victory was and is impossible and will never come. It is, in fact, more than possible. It is something that has arrived in innumerable ways, small and large and often incremental, but not in that way that was widely described and expected. So victories slip by unheralded. Failures are more readily detected.

And then every now and then, the possibilities explode. In these moments of rupture, people find themselves members of a "we" that did not until then exist, at least not as an entity with agency and identity and potency; new possibilities suddenly emerge, or that old dream of a just society reemerges and—at least for a little while—shines. Utopia is sometimes the goal. It's often embedded in the moment itself, and it's a hard moment to explain, since it usually involves hardscrabble ways of living, squabbles, and eventually disillusion and factionalism— but also more ethereal things: the discovery of personal and collective power, the realization of dreams, the birth of bigger dreams, a sense of connection that is as emotional as it is political, and lives that change and do not revert to older ways even when the glory subsides.

Sometimes the earth closes over this moment and it has no obvious consequences; sometimes empires crumble and ideologies fall away like shackles. But you don't know beforehand. People in official institutions devoutly believe they hold the power that matters, though the power we grant them can often be taken back; the violence commanded by governments and militaries often fails, and nonviolent direct-action campaigns often succeed.

The sleeping giant is one name for the public; when it wakes up, when *we* wake up, we are no longer only the public: we are civil society, the superpower whose nonviolent means are sometimes, for a shining moment, more powerful than violence, more powerful than regimes and armies. We write history with our feet and with our presence and our collective voice and vision. And yet, and of course, everything in the mainstream media suggests that popular resistance is ridiculous, pointless, or criminal, unless it is far away, was long ago, or, ideally, both. These are the forces that prefer the giant remain asleep.

Together we are very powerful, and we have a seldom-told, seldom-remembered history of victories and transformations that can give us confidence that yes, we can change the world because we have many times before. You row forward looking back, and telling this history is part of helping people navigate toward the future. We need a litany, a rosary, a sutra, a mantra, a war chant of our victories. The past is set in daylight, and it can become a torch we can carry into the night that is the future.

1

Looking Into Darkness

On January 18, 1915, six months into the First World War, as all Europe was convulsed by killing and dying, Virginia Woolf wrote in her journal, "The future is dark, which is on the whole, the best thing the future can be, I think." Dark, she seems to say, as in inscrutable, not as in terrible. We often mistake the one for the other. Or we transform the future's unknowability into something certain, the fulfillment of all our dread, the place beyond which there is no way forward. But again and again, far stranger things happen than the end of the world.

Who, two decades ago, could have imagined a world in which the Soviet Union had vanished and the Internet had arrived? Who then dreamed that the political prisoner Nelson Mandela would become president of a transformed South Africa? Who foresaw the resurgence of the indigenous world of which the Zapatista uprising in Southern Mexico is only the most visible face? Who, four decades ago, could have conceived of the changed status of all who are nonwhite, nonmale, or nonstraight, the wide-open conversations about power, nature, economies, and ecologies?

There are times when it seems as though not only the future but the present is dark: few recognize what a radically transformed world

1

we live in, one that has been transformed not only by such nightmares as global warming and global capital but by dreams of freedom, of justice, and transformed by things we could not have dreamed of. We adjust to changes without measuring them; we forget how much the culture changed. The US Supreme Court ruled in favor of gay rights on a grand scale in the summer of 2003[1] and in late 2004 refused to re-examine the Massachusetts State Supreme Court ruling affirming the right to same-sex marriage, rulings inconceivable a few decades ago. What accretion of incremental, imperceptible changes made them possible, and how did they come about? And so we need to hope for the realization of our own dreams, but also to recognize a world that will remain wilder than our imaginations.

One June day in 1982, a million people gathered in New York City's Central Park to demand a bilateral nuclear weapons freeze as the first step to disarmament. They didn't get it. The freeze movement was full of people who believed they'd realize their goal in a few years and go back to private life. They were motivated by a storyline in which the world would be made safe, safe for, among other things, going home from activism. Many went home disappointed or burned out, though some are still doing great work. But in less than a decade, major nuclear arms reductions were negotiated, helped along by European antinuclear movements and the impetus they gave the Soviet Union's last president, Mikhail Gorbachev. Since then, the issue has fallen off the map and we have lost much of what was gained. The US Senate refused to ratify the Comprehensive Test Ban Treaty that could have contributed to an end

---

1. On June 26, 2003, the Supreme Court overturned the verdict in *Lawrence v. Texas*, a case in which two Houston residents were arrested and prosecuted under a law criminalizing sex between two men. The court decided the constitutional right to privacy made activity between consenting adults no business of the state. The decision was very different from the court's 1986 decision in *Bowers v. Hardwick*, upholding a Georgia law criminalizing sodomy, as oral and anal sex were Biblically termed.

to nuclear weapons development and proliferation. Instead, the arms race continues as new nations go nuclear, and the current Bush administration is considering resuming the full-fledged nuclear testing halted in 1991, resuming development and manufacture, expanding the arsenal (though Congress defunded the new nuke programs in November 2004), and perhaps even using it in once-proscribed ways. The activism of the freeze era cut itself short with a fixed vision and an unrealistic timeline, not anticipating that the Cold War would come to an end at the end of the decade. They didn't push hard enough or stay long enough to collect the famous peace dividend, and so there was none.

It's always too soon to go home. And it's always too soon to calculate effect. I once read an anecdote by someone in Women Strike for Peace (WSP), the first great antinuclear movement in the United States, the one that did contribute to a major victory: the 1963 Limited Test Ban Treaty, which brought about the end of aboveground testing of nuclear weapons and of much of the radioactive fallout that was showing up in mother's milk and baby teeth. (And WSP contributed to the fall of the House Un-American Activities Committee [HUAC], the Department of Homeland Security of its day. Positioning themselves as housewives and using humor as their weapon, they made HUAC's anticommunist interrogations ridiculous.) The woman from WSP told of how foolish and futile she felt standing in the rain one morning protesting at the Kennedy White House. Years later she heard Dr. Benjamin Spock—who had become one of the most high-profile activists on the issue—say that the turning point for him was spotting a small group of women standing in the rain, protesting at the White House. If they were so passionately committed, he thought, he should give the issue more consideration himself.

Cause-and-effect assumes history marches forward, but history is not an army. It is a crab scuttling sideways, a drip of soft water wearing away stone, an earthquake breaking centuries of tension. Sometimes one person inspires a movement, or her words do decades later; some-

times a few passionate people change the world; sometimes they start a
mass movement and millions do; sometimes those millions are stirred
by the same outrage or the same ideal, and change comes upon us like
a change of weather. All that these transformations have in common is
that they begin in the imagination, in hope. To hope is to gamble. It's
to bet on the future, on your desires, on the possibility that an open
heart and uncertainty is better than gloom and safety. To hope is dangerous, and yet it is the opposite of fear, for to live is to risk.

I say all this because hope is not like a lottery ticket you can sit on
the sofa and clutch, feeling lucky. I say it because hope is an ax you
break down doors with in an emergency; because hope should shove
you out the door, because it will take everything you have to steer
the future away from endless war, from the annihilation of the earth's
treasures and the grinding down of the poor and marginal. Hope just
means another world might be possible, not promised, not guaranteed. Hope calls for action; action is impossible without hope. At the
beginning of his massive 1930s treatise on hope, the German philosopher Ernst Bloch wrote, "The work of this emotion requires people
who throw themselves actively into what is becoming, to which they
themselves belong." To hope is to give yourself to the future, and that
commitment to the future makes the present inhabitable.

Anything could happen, and whether we act or not has everything
to do with it. Though there is no lottery ticket for the lazy and the de-
tached, for the engaged there is a tremendous gamble for the highest
stakes right now. I say this to you not because I haven't noticed that the
United States has strayed close to destroying itself and its purported
values in pursuit of empire in the world and the eradication of democracy at home, that our civilization is close to destroying the very nature
on which we depend—the oceans, the atmosphere, the uncounted species of plant and insect and bird. I say it because I have noticed: wars
will break out, the planet will heat up, species will die out, but how

many, how hot, and what survives depends on whether we act. The future is dark, with a darkness as much of the womb as the grave.

Here, in this book, I want to propose a new vision of how change happens; I want to count a few of the victories that get overlooked; I want to assess the wildly changed world we inhabit; I want to throw out the crippling assumptions that keep many from being a voice in the world. I want to start over, with an imagination adequate to the possibilities and the strangeness and the dangers on this earth in this moment.

2

When We Lost

I n the past couple of years two great waves of despair have come in—or perhaps waves is too energetic a term, since the despair felt like a stall, a becalming, a running aground. The more recent despair was over the presidential election in the United States, as though, the Uruguayan writer Eduardo Galeano commented, George W. Bush was running for President of the World. And he won, despite the opposition of most of the people in the world, despite the polls, despite the fact that a majority of US voters did not choose him—or John Kerry; 40 percent of the electorate stayed home, despite a surge of organization and activism by progressives and leftists who didn't even agree with Kerry on so very much, despite the terrible record of violence and destruction Bush had accrued, despite the stark disaster the Iraq War had become. He won.[2] Which is to say that we lost.

The pain was very real, and it was generous-hearted, felt by many people who would not suffer directly but would see that which they loved—truth, their fellow human beings, as the shut-out in the United

---

2. That the 2000 presidential election was stolen and the 2004 one likely was, at least in Ohio, meant that the fate of the world during those eight years was not the will of the people of the United States, though perhaps it was due to our lack of will to resist these low-impact slow-motion coups.

States or the starving and shot-at in Iraq, the fish in the sea and the trees in the forests—assaulted further. That empathy was generous, and so was the sense of exhaustion—we had imagined taking off the terrible burden that is Bush, and it was painful to resume that leaden weight for four more years. We felt clearly the pain of the circumstances to which we had grown numb.

But the despair was something else again. Sometime before the election was over, I vowed to keep away from what I thought of as "the Conversation," the tailspin of mutual wailing about how bad everything was, a recitation of the evidence against us—one exciting opportunity the left offers is of being your own prosecutor—that just buried any hope and imagination down into a dank little foxhole of curled-up despair. Now I watch people having it, wondering what it is we get from it. The certainty of despair—is even that kind of certainty so worth pursuing? Stories trap us, stories free us, we live and die by stories, but hearing people have the Conversation is hearing them tell themselves a story they believe is being told to them. What other stories can be told? How do people recognize that they have the power to be storytellers, not just listeners? Hope is the story of uncertainty, of coming to terms with the risk involved in not knowing what comes next, which is more demanding than despair and, in a way, more frightening. And immeasurably more rewarding. What strikes you when you come out of a deep depression or get close to a depressed person is the utter self-absorption of misery. Which is why the political imagination is better fueled by looking deeper and farther. The larger world: it was as though it disappeared during that season, as though there were only two places left on earth: Iraq, like hell on earth, and the United States, rotting from the center. The United States is certainly the center of the world's military might, and its war in the heart of the Arab world for control of the global oil supply matters a lot. The suffering of people in Iraq matters and so do the deaths of more than a hundred thousand of them, along with, at this writing, more than 1,500 Americans and 76 Britons. This is where the future is being clubbed over the head.

But I think the future is being invented in South America.[3] When I think about elections in the autumn of 2004, I think of them as a trio. In Uruguay, after not four years of creepy governments but a hundred and seventy years—ever since Victoria was a teenage queen—the people got a good leftist government. As Eduardo Galeano joyfully wrote,

> A few days before the election of the President of the planet in North America, in South America elections and a plebiscite were held in a little-known, almost secret country called Uruguay. In these elections, for the first time in the country's history, the left won. And in the plebiscite, for the first time in world history, the privatization of water was rejected by popular vote, asserting that water is the right of all people . . . The country is unrecognizable. Uruguayans, so unbelieving that even nihilism was beyond them, have started to believe, and with fervor. And today this melancholic and subdued people, who at first glance might be Argentineans on valium, are dancing on air. The winners have a tremendous burden of responsibility. This rebirth of faith and revival of happiness must be watched over carefully. We should recall every day

3. The rise of progressive Latin American governments was a beautiful thing. But after victory comes more change. As Uruguayan political observer Raoul Zibechi noted in 2015: "Progressivism in Latin America, which broke out around 10 or 15 years ago depending on which country you're talking about, produced some positive changes. But I think that cycle has come to an end. While there continue to be progressive governments, what I am saying is that progressivism as a set of political forces that created something relatively positive: this has ended . . . Progressivism in Latin America stands at a crossroads: either it changes into a political movement advocating real change reaching the structures of society—ownership of land, tax reform targeting the rich—or these governments simply become conservative, which is a process I think has already begun." It might be added that much of the progressivism of the region was never governmental and isn't over.

how right Carlos Quijano was when he said that sins against hope are the only sins beyond forgiveness and redemption.

In Chile, shortly after the US election, huge protests against the Bush administration and its policies went on for several days. Maybe Chile is the center of the world; maybe the fact that they went from a terrifying military dictatorship under Pinochet to a democracy where people can be outspoken in their passion for justice on the other side of the world is indicative too. As longtime Chile observer Roger Burbach wrote after those demonstrations, "There is indeed a Chilean alternative to Bush: it is to pursue former dictators and the real terrorists by using international law and building a global international criminal system that will be based on an egalitarian economic system that empowers people at the grass roots to build their own future." A month later, Chile succeeded where Britain had failed: Pinochet was put on trial for his crimes. And in a US-backed referendum in August 2004, Venezuelans again voted a landslide victory to the target of an unsuccessful US-backed coup in 2002, left-wing populist president Hugo Chavez. That spring, Argentina's current president, Nestor Kirchner, backed by the country's popular rebellion against neoliberalism, boldly defied the International Monetary Fund (IMF).[4] The year before, Bolivians fought against natural gas privatization so fiercely they chased their neoliberal president into exile in Miami not long after Brazil, under the rule of Luiz Inácio "Lula" da Silva, led the developing world in a revolt against the World Trade Organization. South America was neoliberalism's great laboratory, and now it's the site of the greatest revolts against that pernicious economic doctrine (which might be most tersely defined as

4. South Americans would almost completely banish the International Monetary Fund and its policy impositions from their continent. Between 2005 and 2007, Latin America went from taking on 80 percent of the IMF's treacherous, conditions-laden loans to 1 percent. The transformation was made possible in part by loans to several countries in the region from oil-rich Venezuela.

the cult of unfettered international capitalism and privatization of goods and services behind what gets called globalization—and might more accurately be called corporate globalization and the commodification of absolutely everything).

Which is not to say, forget Iraq, forget the United States, just to say, remember Uruguay, remember Chile, remember Venezuela, remember the extraordinary movements against privatization and for justice, democracy, land reform, and indigenous rights in Brazil, Bolivia, Ecuador, and Argentina. Not one or the other, but both. South America is important because these communities are inventing a better politics of means and of ends. That continent is also important because twenty years or so ago, almost all those countries were run by malevolent dictators. We know how the slide into tyranny and fear takes place, how people fall into a nightmare, but how do they wake up from it, how does the slow climb back into freedom and confidence transpire? That road to recovery is something worth thinking about, because Bush is halfway through an eight-year term, not at the start of a thousand-year reich, so far as we can tell.

For history will remember 2004 not with the microscopic lens of we who lived through it the way aphids traverse a rose, but with a telescopic eye that sees it as part of the stream of wild changes of the past few decades, some for the worse, some for the better. And even 2004 was far broader than the US election: not only did Uruguay have its first great election, but the Ukraine had its electoral upset. Massive voter fraud, dioxin poisoning, media manipulation, and the long arms of the Kremlin and the CIA hardly made for an ideal situation, but the brave resistance, camping out in the streets, chanting and dancing and pushing its way into the parliament, nicely echoed the Central European movements against the then-communist state fifteen years before. More importantly, the nearly one billion citizens of India managed to kick out the Bharatiya Janata Party, with its strange mix of Hindu racism and cultic neoliberalism. Afterward, Arundhati Roy said, "For many of us who feel estranged from mainstream politics, there are rare, ephemeral moments of celebration." And there is far more to politics than the mainstream of elections and governments, more in the margins where hope is most at home.

This is what the world usually looks like, not like Uruguay last fall, not like the United States, but like both. F. Scott Fitzgerald famously said, "The test of a first-rate intelligence is the ability to hold two opposed ideas in the mind at the same time, and still retain the ability to function," but the summations of the state of the world often assume that it must be all one way or the other, and since it is not all good it must all suck royally. Fitzgerald's forgotten next sentence is, "One should, for example, be able to see that things are hopeless and yet be determined to make them otherwise." You wonder what made Vaclav Havel hopeful in 1985 or 1986, when Czechoslovakia was still a Soviet satellite and he was still a jailbird playwright.

Havel said then,

> The kind of hope I often think about (especially in situations that are particularly hopeless, such as prison) I understand above all as a state of mind, not a state of the world. Either we have hope within us or we don't; it is a dimension of the soul; it's not essentially dependent on some particular observation of the world or estimate of the situation. Hope is not prognostication. It is an orientation of the spirit, an orientation of the heart; it transcends the world that is immediately experienced, and is anchored somewhere beyond its horizons. Hope, in this deep and powerful sense, is not the same as joy that things are going well, or willingness to invest in enterprises that are obviously headed for early success, but, rather, an ability to work for something because it is good, not just because it stands a chance to succeed.

Hope and action feed each other. There are people with good grounds for despair and a sense of powerlessness: prisoners, the desperately poor, those overwhelmed by the labors of just surviving, those living under the threat of imminent violence. And there are less tangible reasons for inaction. When I think back to why I was apolitical into my mid-twenties I see that being politically engaged means having a sense of your own power—that what you do matters—and a sense of belonging, things that came to me only later and that do not come to all. Overcoming alienation and isolation or their causes is a political goal for the rest of us. And for the rest of us, despair is more a kind of fatigue, a loss of faith, that can be overcome, or even an indulgence if you look at the power of being political as a privilege not granted to everyone. And it's that rest of us I'll continue railing at—though sometimes it's the most unlikely people who rise up and take power, the housewives who are supposed to be nobody, the prisoners who organize from inside, the people who have an intimate sense of what's at stake. You can frame it another way. The revolutionary Brazilian educator Paolo Freire wrote a sequel to his famous *Pedagogy of the Oppressed* called *Pedagogy of Hope*, and in it he declares, "Without a minimum of hope, we cannot so much as start the struggle. But without the struggle, hope dissipates, loses its bearings, and turns into hopelessness. And hopelessness can turn into tragic despair. Hence the need for a kind of education in hope."

The despair that keeps coming up is a loss of belief that the struggle is worthwhile. That loss comes from many quarters: from exhaustion, from a sadness born out of empathy, but also from expectations and analyses that are themselves problems. "Resistance is the secret of joy," said a banner carried by Reclaim the Streets in the late 1990s, quoting Alice Walker. Resistance is first of all a matter of principle and a way to live, to make yourself one small republic of unconquered spirit. You hope for results, but you don't depend on them. And if you study the historical record, there have been results, as surprising as Czechoslovakia's 1989 Velvet Revolution, and there will be more, though they are in the dark, beyond what can be expected. And as

Freire points out, struggle generates hope as it goes along. Waiting until everything looks feasible is too long to wait.

This book tells stories of victories and possibilities because the defeats and disasters are more than adequately documented; it exists not in opposition to or denial of them, but in symbiosis with them, or perhaps as a small counterweight to their tonnage. In the past half century, the state of the world has declined dramatically, measured by material terms and by the brutality of wars and ecological onslaughts. But we have also added a huge number of intangibles, of rights, ideas, concepts, words to describe and to realize what was once invisible or unimaginable, and these constitute both a breathing space and a toolbox, a toolbox with which those atrocities can be and have been addressed, a box of hope.

I want to illuminate a past that is too seldom recognized, one in which the power of individuals and unarmed people is colossal, in which the scale of change in the world and the collective imagination over the past few decades is staggering, in which the astonishing things that have taken place can brace us for entering that dark future with boldness. To recognize the momentousness of what has happened is to apprehend what might happen. Inside the word *emergency* is *emerge*; from an emergency new things come forth. The old certainties are crumbling fast, but danger and possibility are sisters.

3

What We Won

What prompted me to start writing about hope was the first wave of despair, the one that followed a season of extraordinary peace activism in the spring of 2003. The despairing could only recognize one victory, the one we didn't grasp, the prevention of the war in Iraq. The Bush and Blair administrations suggested that the taking of Baghdad constituted victory, but the real war began then, the guerrilla resistance and the international fallout that will long be felt. By the fall of 2003, we had been vindicated in our refusal to believe that Saddam Hussein's regime posed a serious threat to the United States, the UK, or the world, or harbored serious arsenals of weapons of mass destruction. By the winter of 2004, few members of the bullied minor nations known as the "coalition of the willing" remained, we were in quicksand, and hardly anyone bothered to argue there had been a good reason for jumping into it. But being right is small comfort when people are dying and living horribly, as are both the Iraqis in their ravaged land and the poor kids who constitute our occupying army.

At the same time, the peace movement that erupted so spectacularly in 2003 accomplished some significant things that need to be recognized. We will likely never know, but it seems that the Bush administration decided against the "shock and awe" saturation bombing of Baghdad because we made it clear that the cost in world opinion and civil unrest would be too high. We millions may have saved a few thousand or a few tens of thousands of lives. The global debate about the war delayed it for months, months that perhaps gave many Iraqis time to lay in stores, evacuate, brace for the onslaught.

Activists are often portrayed as an unrepresentative, marginal rabble, but something shifted in the media in the fall of 2002. Since then, antiwar activists have mostly been represented as a diverse, legitimate, and representative body, a victory for our representation and our long-term prospects. Many people who had never spoken out, never marched in the street, never joined groups, written to politicians, or donated to campaigns, did so; countless people became political as never before. That is, if nothing else, a vast reservoir of passion now stored up to feed the river of change. New networks and communities and websites and listservs and jail solidarity groups and coalitions arose and are still with us.

In the name of the so-called War on Terror, which seems to inculcate terror at home and enact it abroad, we were encouraged to fear our neighbors, each other, strangers (particularly Middle Eastern, Arab, and Muslim people or people who looked that way), to spy on them, to lock ourselves up, to privatize ourselves. By living out our hope and resistance in public together with strangers of all kinds, we overcame this catechism of fear, we trusted each other; we forged a community that bridged the differences among the peace-loving as we demonstrated our commitment to the people of Iraq.

We achieved a global movement without leaders. There were brilliant spokespeople, theorists and organizers, but when your fate rests on your leader, you are only as strong, as incorruptible, and as creative as he—or, occasionally, she—is. What could be more democratic than millions of people who, via the grapevine, the Internet, and various assemblies from churches to unions to direct-action affinity groups, can organize themselves? Of course leaderless actions and movements have been organized for the past couple of decades, but never on such a grand scale. The African writer Laurens Van Der Post once said that no great new leaders were emerging because it was time for us to cease to be followers. Perhaps we have.

Most of us succeeded in refusing the dichotomies. We were able to oppose a war on Iraq without endorsing Saddam Hussein. We were able to oppose a war with compassion for the troops who fought it. Most of us did not fall into the traps that our foreign policy so often does and that earlier generations of radicals sometimes did: the ones in which our enemy's enemy is our friend, in which the opponent of an evil must be good, in which a nation and its figurehead, a general and his troops, become indistinguishable. We were not against the United States and UK and for the Baathist regime or the insurgency; we were against the war, and many of us were against all war, all weapons of mass destruction, and all violence, everywhere. We are not just an antiwar movement. We are a peace movement.

Questions the peace and global justice movements have raised are now mainstream, though no mainstream source will say why, or perhaps even knows why. Activists targeted Bechtel, Halliburton, Chevron-Texaco, and Lockheed Martin, among others, as war profiteers with ties to the Bush administration. The actions worked not just by shutting places down but by making their operations a public question. Direct action is indirectly powerful: now the media scrutinizes those corporations as never before, and their names are widely known.

Gary Younge writes in the *Guardian*,

> The antiwar movement got the German chancellor, Gerhard Schröder, re-elected, and has pushed the center of gravity in the Democratic primaries in a more progressive direction. Political leaders need not only geographical but also ideological constituencies. Over the past two years the left has built a strong enough base to support those who chose to challenge American hegemony.

True, none of this has saved Iraqi lives. But with ratings for Bush and Blair plummeting, it may keep Iranians, North Koreans or whoever else they are considering bombing out of harm's way.

Even Canada and Mexico distanced themselves from the United States, as though they could make the center of the continent the island it is in diplomatic terms. Despite a huge open bribe, because of the outcry of countless Turkish citizens, the Turkish government refused to let the invaders of Iraq use Turkey as a staging ground. And many other nations arrived at a stance on the war that was driven by public opinion, not by strategic advantage. The war we got was not the war that would have transpired with universal public acquiescence.

None of these victories are comparable to the victory that preventing the war would have been—but if the war had indeed been canceled, the Bush and Blair administrations would have supplied elaborate reasons that had nothing to do with public opinion and international pressure, and many would still believe that we had no impact. The government and the media routinely discount the effect of activists, but there's no reason we should believe them or let them tally our victories for us. To be effective, activists have to make strong, simple, urgent demands, at least some of the time—the kind of demands that fit on stickers and placards, the kind that can be shouted in the street by a thousand people. And they have to recognize that their victories may come as subtle, complex, slow changes instead, and count them anyway. A gift for embracing paradox is not the least of the equipment an activist should have.

And there's one more victory worth counting. The scale and scope of the global peace movement was grossly underreported on February 15, 2003, when somewhere between twelve and thirty million people marched and demonstrated, on every continent, including the scientists at MacMurdo Station in Antarctica. A million people marching in Barcelona was nice, but I also heard about the thousands in Chapel Hill, North Carolina, the hundred and fifty people holding a peace vigil in the small town of Las Vegas, New Mexico, the antiwar passion of people in even smaller villages in Bolivia, in Thailand, in Inuit northern Canada. George W. Bush campaigned as a uniter, not a divider, and he very nearly united the whole world against the administrations of the United States and Britain. Those tens of millions worldwide constituted something unprecedented, one of the ruptures that have ushered in a new era. They are one reason to hope for the future.

4

False Hope
and Easy Despair

I n his book *The Principle of Hope*, Ernst Bloch declares, "Fraudulent hope is one of the greatest malefactors, even enervators, of the human race, concretely genuine hope its most dedicated benefactor" and speaks of "informed discontent which belongs to hope, because they both arise out of the No to deprivation." When I think of the recent US presidential election, I think of Bush's constant deployment of false hope—that we were going to win the war in Iraq, that his wars had made US citizens and the world safer, that the domestic economy was doing fine (and that the environment is not even a subject for discussion). Perhaps *hope* is the wrong word for these assertions, not that another world is possible, but that it is unnecessary, that everything is fine—now go back to sleep. Such speech aims to tranquilize and disempower the populace, to keep us isolated and at home, seduced into helplessness, just as more direct tyrannies seek to terrify citizens into isolation.

The Bush administration uses fear too, and it's interesting that those urbanites who have been at risk—of nuclear annihilation during the Cold War, of assault during the crime-ridden 1980s, of being targeted by terrorism nowadays, insofar as terrorism is a meaningful risk at all—have been among the least fearful. Instead, people who are already isolated in suburbs and other alienated landscapes, far from crime, outside key targets for war or terror, are far more vulnerable to these fears, which seem not false but displaced. That is to say, the fear is real, but its putative subject is false. In this sense, it is a safe fear, since to acknowledge the real sources of fear might itself be frightening, calling for radical questioning, radical change. This, I think, is how false hope and false fear become such a neat carrot and stick luring the democratic beast along to its own demise.

Bush invited his constituency to be blind to the world's real problems, and leftists often do the opposite, gazing so fixedly at those problems that they cannot see beyond them. Thus it is that the world often seems divided between false hope and gratuitous despair. Despair demands less of us, it's more predictable, and in a sad way safer. Authentic hope requires clarity—seeing the troubles in this world—and imagination, seeing what might lie beyond these situations that are perhaps not inevitable and immutable.

Left despair has many causes and many varieties. There are those who think that turning the official version inside out is enough. To say that the emperor has no clothes is a nice antiauthoritarian gesture, but to say that everything without exception is going straight to hell is not an alternative vision but only an inverted version of the mainstream's "everything's fine." Then, failure and marginalization are safe—you can see the conservatives who run the United States claim to be embattled outsiders, because that means they can deny their responsibility for how things are and their power to make change, and because it is a sense of being threatened that rallies their troops. The activists who deny their own power and possibility likewise choose to shake off their sense of obligation: if they are doomed to lose, they don't have to do very much except situate themselves as beautiful losers or at least virtuous ones.

There are the elaborate theory hawkers, who invest their opponents with superhuman abilities that never falter and can never be successfully resisted—they seem obsessed with an enemy that never lets them go, though the enemy is in part their own fantasy and its fixity. There are those who see despair as solidarity with the oppressed, though the oppressed may not particularly desire that version of themselves, since they may have had a life before being victims and might hope to have one after. And gloom is not much of a gift. Then there are those whose despair is personal in origin, projected outward as political analysis. This is often coupled with nostalgia for a time that may never have existed or may have been terrible for some, a location in which all that is broken now can be imagined to have once been whole. It is a way around introspection.

Another motive for gloom is grandstanding, for the bearer of bad news is less likely to get shot than to acquire a certain authority that those bringing better or more complicated news won't. Fire, brimstone and impending apocalypse have always had great success in the pulpit, and the apocalypse is always easier to imagine than the strange circuitous routes to what actually comes next. And then, speaking of fire, there is burnout, the genuine exhaustion of those who tried—though sometimes they tried in ways guaranteed to lead to frustration or defeat (and then, sometimes, they burned out from being surrounded by all these other versions of left despair, to say nothing of infighting).

Sometimes the commitment to the gloomy version becomes comical. From the 1960s onward, people worried about "the population bomb," the Malthusian theory that global population would increase without any check short of resource and health disasters. Sometime in the 1990s, it became clear that birthrates in many parts of the world were decreasing, that globally population would peak—in about 2025, according to current estimates—then decline. Nations of the industrialized world, where resource consumption is highest, including Japan, Canada, Australia, Europe, and Russia, are already on the downswing. Rather than celebrate that an old problem had gone away of itself (or of changed social circumstances, including the spread of women's reproductive rights), declining population is often framed as a new impending crisis. The situation had changed completely, but the song remained the same.

The focus on survival demands that you notice the tiger in the tree before you pay attention to the beauty of its branches. The one person who's furious at you compels more attention than the eighty-nine who love you. Problems are our work; we deal with them in order to survive or to improve the world, and so to face them is better than turning away from them, from burying them and denying them. To face them can be an act of hope, but only if you remember that they're not all there is.

Hope is not a door, but a sense that there might be a door at some point, some way out of the problems of the present moment even before that way is found or followed. Sometimes radicals settle for excoriating the wall for being so large, so solid, so blank, so without hinges, knobs, keyholes, rather than seeking a door, or they trudge through a door looking for a new wall. Hope, Ernst Bloch adds, is in love with success rather than failure, and I'm not sure that's true of a lot of the most audible elements of the left. The only story many leftists know how to tell is the story that is the underside of the dominant culture's story, more often than the stuff that never makes it into the news, and all news has a bias in favor of suddenness, violence, and disaster that overlooks groundswells, sea changes, and alternatives, the forms in which popular power most often manifests itself. Their gloomy premise is that the powers that be are not telling you the whole truth, but the truth they tell is also incomplete. They conceive of the truth as pure bad news, appoint themselves the deliverers of it, and keep telling it over and over. Eventually, they come to look for the downside in any emerging story, even in apparent victories—and in each other: something about this task seems to give some of them the souls of meter maids and dogcatchers. (Of course, this also has to do with the nature of adversarial activism, which leads to obsession with the enemy, and, as a few environmentalists have mentioned to me, with the use of alarmist narratives for fundraising and mobilizing.)

Sometimes these bad-news bringers seem in love with defeat, because if they're constantly prophesying doom, actual doom is, as we say in California, pretty validating. They come to own the bad and even take pride in it: the monsters and atrocities prove their point, and the point is very dear to them. But part of it is a personal style: I think that this grimness is more a psychology than an ideology. There's a kind of activism that's more about bolstering identity than achieving results, one that sometimes seems to make the left the true heirs of the Puritans. Puritanical in that the point becomes the demonstration of one's own virtue rather than the realization of results. And puritanical because the somber pleasure of condemning things is the most enduring part of that legacy, along with the sense of personal superiority that comes from pleasure denied. The bleakness of the world is required as contrasting backdrop to the drama of their rising above.

Despair, bad news, and grimness bolster an identity the teller can affect, one that is tough enough to face the facts. Some of them, anyway. (Some of the facts remain in the dark.) The outcome is usually uncertain, but for some reason tales of decline and fall have an authority that hopeful ones don't. Buddhists sometimes decry hope as an attachment to a specific outcome, to a story line, to satisfaction. But beyond that is an entirely different sort of hope: that you possess the power to change the world to some degree or just that the world is going to change again, and uncertainty and instability thereby become grounds for hope.

Walls can justify being stalled; doors demand passage. Hopefulness is risky, since it is after all a form of trust, trust in the unknown and the possible, even in discontinuity. To be hopeful is to take on a different persona, one that risks disappointment, betrayal, and there have been major disappointments in recent years. Other times that tale of gloom seems to come from the belief in a univocal narrative, in the idea that everything is heading in one direction, and since it's clearly not all good, it must be bad. "Democracy is in trouble" is the phrase with which an eminent activist opens a talk, which is true, but it's also true that it's flourishing in bold new ways in grassroots movements globally.

It's important to denounce the wall, to describe its obdurate impenetrability. Before a disease can be treated, it must be diagnosed. And you do not need to know the prescription before you diagnose a disease. Thus it is that telling the bad news can be a gift and a step toward hope, as long as that news can be let go when the time comes or the world changes. But you have to be able to see farther, to look elsewhere.

Political awareness without activism means looking at the devastation, your face turned toward the center of things. Activism itself can generate hope because it already constitutes an alternative and turns away from the corruption at center to face the wild possibilities and the heroes at the edges or at your side. These ideas of hope are deeply disturbing to a certain kind of presumptive progressive, one who is securely established one way or another. It may be simply that this is not their story, or it may be that hope demands things of them despair does not. Sometimes they regard stories of victory or possibility as hard-hearted. Another part of the Puritan legacy is the belief that no one should have joy or abundance until everyone does, a belief that's austere at one end, in the deprivation it endorses, and fantastical in the other, since it awaits a universal utopia. Joy sneaks in anyway, abundance cascades forth uninvited. The great human rights activist and Irish nationalist Roger Casement investigated horrific torture and genocide in South America's Putamayo rainforest a century ago and campaigned to end it. While on this somber task, his journal reveals, he found time to admire handsome local men and to chase brilliantly colored local butterflies. Joy doesn't betray but sustains activism. And when you face a politics that aspires to make you fearful, alienated, and isolated, joy is a fine initial act of insurrection.

5

A History of Shadows

Imagine the world as a theater. The acts of the powerful and the official occupy center stage. The traditional versions of history, the conventional sources of news encourage us to fix our gaze on that stage. The limelights there are so bright that they blind you to the shadowy spaces around you, make it hard to meet the gaze of the other people in the seats, to see the way out of the audience, into the aisles, backstage, outside, in the dark, where other powers are at work. A lot of the fate of the world is decided onstage, in the limelight, and the actors there will tell you that all of it is, that there is no other place.

No matter the details or the outcome, what is onstage is a tragedy, the tragedy of the inequitable distribution of power, the tragedy of the too common silence of those who settle for being audience and who pay the price of the drama. The idea behind representative democracy is that the audience is supposed to choose the actors, and the actors are quite literally supposed to speak for us. In practice, various reasons keep many from participating in the choice, other forces—like money—subvert that choice, and onstage too many of the actors find other reasons—lobbyists, self-interest, conformity—to fail to represent their constituents.

Pay attention to the inventive arenas that exert political power outside that stage or change the contents of the drama onstage. From the places that you have been instructed to ignore or rendered unable to see come the stories that change the world, and it is here that culture has the power to shape politics and ordinary people have the power to change the world. You can see the baffled, upset faces of the actors on stage when the streets become a stage or the unofficial appear among them to disrupt the planned program.

A month or two before the Bush and Blair administrations began bombing Baghdad, Jonathan Schell published *The Unconquerable World: Power, Nonviolence, and the Will of the People*. The book eloquently argues for a new idea of change and of power. One of its key recognitions is that the change that counts in revolution takes place first in the imagination. Histories usually pick up when the action begins, but Schell quotes John Adams saying that the American Revolution "was in the minds of the people and in the union of the colonies, both of which were accomplished before hostilities commenced." And Thomas Jefferson concluded, "This was effected from 1760 to 1775, in the course of fifteen years, before a drop of blood was shed at Lexington."

This means, of course, that the most foundational change of all, the one from which all else issues, is hardest to track. It means that politics arises out of the spread of ideas and the shaping of imaginations. It means that symbolic and cultural acts have real political power. And it means that the changes that count take place not merely onstage as action but in the minds of those who are again and again pictured only as audience or bystanders. The revolution that counts is the one that takes place in the imagination; many kinds of change issue forth thereafter, some gradual and subtle, some dramatic and conflict-ridden—which is to say that revolution doesn't necessarily look like revolution.

Schell describes how the United States lost the war in Vietnam because, despite extraordinary military superiority, it could not win over the people of that country and finally lost the confidence and support of its own citizens: "In the new world of politically committed and active people, it was not force per se but the collective wills of those peoples that were decisive." In other words, belief can be more effective than violence. Violence is the power of the state; imagination and nonviolence the power of civil society.

Nonviolence, Schell argues, has in the last century become an increasingly powerful force in the world, a counterforce to war and to violence, and with that more and more power has come to belong to the ordinary citizenry. His claim was mocked during the opening salvos of the Iraq War but that quagmire of a war and the opposition to it around the world have strengthened his case. It's an immensely hopeful position, identifying the rise of nonviolence and the importance of its role not just in Gandhi's India or King's South but in places where few noticed. (Among other recent successes of nonviolent direct action, Belgrade students toppled Milosevic with patient direct action in the streets of their city, achieving what international powers had failed to do; mostly indigenous Bolivian peasants ousted their president; Puerto Ricans kicked the US Navy out of Vieques; and giant street demonstrations in Mexico undermined privatization of pensions and energy.) It is a reminder of our power to make the world. Schell continues,

> Individual hearts and minds change; those who have been changed become aware of one another; still others are emboldened, in a contagion of boldness; the "impossible" becomes possible; immediately it is done, surprising the actors almost as much as their opponents; and suddenly, almost with the swiftness of thought—whose transformation has in fact set the whole process in motion—the old regime, a moment ago so impressive, vanishes like a mirage.

A literature of hope is gathering these days. In 1785, no one in Britain was thinking about slavery, except slaves, ex-slaves, and a few Quakers and soft-hearted evangelicals. In his 2005 book *Bury the Chains*, Adam Hochschild tells the story of how the dozen or so original activists gathered at a London printer's shop at 2 George Yard, near what is now the Bank tube stop. From that point onward this handful of hopefuls created a movement that in half a century abolished slavery in the British Empire and helped spark the abolition movement that ended slavery in the United States a quarter century or so later. Part of the story is about the imagination and determination of a few key figures. But part of it is about a change of heart whereby enough people came to believe that slavery was an intolerable cruelty to bring its day to an end, despite the profitability of the institution to the powerful who defended it. It was arguments, sermons, editorials, pamphlets, conversations that changed the mind of the public: stories, for the decisions were mostly made in London (encouraged by witnesses and slave revolts abroad). The atrocities were mostly out of sight of the audience. It required imagination, empathy, and information to make abolition a cause and then a victory. In those five decades antislavery sentiments went from being radical to being the status quo.

Stories move faster in our own time. It has taken less than forty years for homosexuality to go from being classified as a crime and a mental disorder to being widely accepted as part of the variety of ordinary, everyday life—and though there is a backlash, backlashes for all their viciousness cannot turn back the clock or put the genie back in his lamp. Polls suggest that homophobia is more a property of the old than the young, that society will gradually shed it, is shedding it, as the generations pass. Like views of slavery, the change comes so incrementally it can only be measured in court decisions and opinion polls, but it did not come as naturally as a change in the weather. It was *made*, by activists, but also by artists, writers, comedians, and filmmakers who asserted other versions of sexuality, other kinds of family, by all those parade organizers and marchers, by millions of ordinary individuals living openly as gay or lesbian, out to their families and communities, by people leaving behind their fears and animosities. Along similar lines, shifts in thought that led to activism and then shifts in law have radically revised the life and rights of the disabled.

You may be told that the legal decisions lead the changes, that judges and lawmakers lead the culture in those theaters called courtrooms, but they only ratify change. They are almost never where change begins, only where it ends up, for most changes travel from the edges to the center. (There was one member of Parliament who steadfastly introduced antislavery legislation in the late eighteenth century; there were parliamentarians and a few congresspeople who opposed the current war, but the opposition was far stronger outside.) You could say that the figures onstage are the actors—or puppets, since much of the script is written elsewhere, out of sight, by corporations and elites, but also by popular movements that tug the conscience and change the status quo, and it is in these neglected places that radical power lies. There and in the circuitous routes to the center, where these new ideas cease to be new as they become the script for the actors onstage, who believe they wrote them. (Stalin reputedly once said, "Ideas are far more dangerous than guns. We don't allow our enemies to have guns, why should we allow them to have ideas?")

How did these stories and beliefs migrate from the margins to the center? Is there a kind of story food chain or dispersal pattern? Can stories be imagined as spreading like viruses or evolving like species to other habitats and other forms? You could even argue that stories spread like fire, except that fire is perhaps the ultimate drama, and stories sneak in while no one is watching. Just as fashions are more likely to originate in the street with poor nonwhite kids, so are new stories likely to start in the marginal zones, with visionaries, radicals, obscure researchers, the young, the poor—the discounted, who count anyway. The routes to the center are seldom discussed or even explored, in part because so much attention is focused on that central stage.

To be pushed to the edges is to be marginalized; to push your way back to the center is often to be defamed and criminalized. The edges are literally marginal—the margins—but they are also portrayed as dangerous and unsavory. One of the great shocks of recent years came to me in a police station in Scotland, where in the course of reporting a lost wallet I found myself contemplating a poster of wanted criminals: not rapists and murderers but kids with peculiar hairstyles and piercings who had been active in demonstrations such as the Carnival Against Capital and other frolics in which business as usual had been disrupted but no one had been harmed. So these were the criminals who most threatened the state? Then the state was fragile and we were powerful.

These days I find myself using the term "safe dangers" for the easy targets onto which people displace their fears, since the true content of their fears may be unsavory or unsettling. In the United States, the Bush administration, the mainstream media, and many mayors and chiefs of police have portrayed as terrorists—as bomb planters, acid-throwers, police assailants—activists employing the First Amendment's guarantee of the right to speak and assemble and the nonviolent tactics of Gandhi and King. Other governments—notably Britain's with those wanted posters and the 1994 Criminal Justice Act—have done the same. They willfully, if not consciously, mistake what kind of danger these street activists pose, as they have before, when civil rights advocates, suffragists, abolitionists were being persecuted. To admit that these people pose a threat to the status quo is to admit first that there is a status quo, secondly that it may be an unjust and unjustifiable thing, and thirdly that it can indeed be changed by passionate people and nonviolent means. To admit this is to admit the limits of state power and its legitimacy. Better to marginalize activists—to portray them as rabble on the fringe who are dangerous the way violent criminals are dangerous. Thus is the true danger to the status quo made into another "safe fear." Thus are both the power and the legitimacy of the margins denied. Denied by those in the limelight, but you don't have to believe them.

I used to. Thinking about how things that once seemed impossibly distant came to pass, I am embarrassed to remember how dismissive of the margins I once was, fifteen or so years ago, when I secretly scoffed at the shantytowns built on college campuses as part of the antiapartheid movement. That people were protesting something so remote and entrenched seemed futile. But then the divestment of college funds from corporations doing business with South Africa became a big part of the sanctions movement, and the sanctions movement prodded along the end of apartheid. What lies ahead seems unlikely; when it becomes the past, it seems inevitable. In 1900, the idea that women should have the vote was revolutionary; now, the idea that we should not have it would seem cracked. But no one went back to apologize to the suffragists who chained themselves to the gates of power, smashed all the windows on Bond Street, spent long months in jail, suffered forced feedings and demonization in the press.

I thought about this again when I was reading a superb story on the Pennsylvania townships seeking to abolish corporate personhood—the legal status that gives corporations a dangerous and undemocratic range of rights in the United States. It seemed like one of those ideas that might be migrating toward the center, but in ten years if *Time* magazine is questioning the shift from democracy to a sort of monarchy of corporations or the *New York Times* is reporting the overturning of the legal principles on which corporate hegemony rests, they won't thank a bunch of radical professors or scruffy anticapitalist street activists who were being tear-gassed for arguing the point prematurely. There will never be a moment when someone in the Senate or on national TV news will say, "Those freaks in the underbrush saw the future when we on high were blind." Instead, the perils of corporate personhood will become common sense, become what everyone always knew. Which is to say, stories migrate secretly. The assumption that whatever we now believe is just common sense, or what we always knew, is a way to save face. It's also a way to forget the power of a story and of a storyteller, the power in the margins, and the potential for change.

Thirty years ago, Edward Abbey wrote a novel, *The Monkey Wrench Gang*, in which his hero blows up Glen Canyon Dam, the huge desert dam strangling the Colorado River upstream from the Grand Canyon. Getting rid of the dam was an outrageous idea then, though the novel helped spark the birth of the radical environmental organization Earth First! In 1981, the group announced its existence by running a three-hundred-foot sheet of plastic, bearing the image of a mighty crack, down the dam, which never seemed quite so eternal and immutable again.

Recently, the idea of taking down the dam, built amid controversy from 1956 to 1963, has come to seem more and more reasonable, more and more likely (the fact that global warming or long-term drought has dropped the reservoir water level to 37 percent capacity doesn't hurt either). More than 145 smaller US dams have already been dismantled, and dams have come down across Europe; the new era has already begun to slip in quietly. The behemoth new dams in China and India are bureaucrats' attempts to catch up to an era already going or gone.

One of the stories my friend Chip Ward follows in his book *Hope's Horizon* is how the idea of dismantling Glen Canyon Dam is gaining support. If it happens, it will come to look like it always was a good idea, and the first people to have espoused it will be forgotten, since they were kooks, extremists, and impractical dreamers. No one in the center will remember when they supported what now looks like bad science and bad engineering, just as few remember when they supported racial segregation or bans on mixed-race marriages. Their amnesia is necessary to their sense of legitimacy in a society they would rather not acknowledge is in constant change.

Chip wrote me the other day,

> As an activist, I have observed that if a story is controversial in nature and threatens the powerful I may have to "inoculate" it first by giving it to a young journalist who has more tolerance for

risk from some alternative weekly that is also more edgy. The next step up the food chain may be a public radio station. After the story appears and the homework is done, if nobody is sued, then I can get a reporter from an established newspaper to write about it or get a television reporter on it. This is partly because newspaper reporters have to convince editors who are a skittish bunch who answer to suits who have their eyes on advertisers and the corporate guys over them who play golf with the people who may be criticized in the story.

This certainly does seem like a food chain, though a food chain in reverse, perhaps, since the television networks are, in Chip's view, eating the alternative media's excretions.

Chip, incidentally, moved to Utah and eventually became one of that state's most powerful environmental activists because his brother-in-law read another Ed Abbey book, *Desert Solitaire*, moved there himself, and sent back reports of how glorious were the red-rock canyons. And so Abbey, who was never much of an activist himself (and was pretty stupid about race and immigration), played a huge role in prompting some of the fiercest activists of our time.

And the group whose creation Abbey helped to inspire spawned a British branch of Earth First! that metamorphosed into the powerful antiroads movement of the mid-1990s, perhaps the most successful direct-action campaign in recent British history. More than five hundred road-building schemes were canceled. And from the antiroads movement came Reclaim the Streets, which sparked many of the creative tactics and attitudes that gave the Northern Hemisphere something to contribute to the movement against corporate globalization at the end of the 1990s and changed the face of activism. Abbey's books weren't the only seeds for these transformations, and it's only because they aren't so deep in the shadows that their influence can be traced; beyond them are countless other sources for change.

Stories move in from the shadows to the limelight. And though the stage presents the drama of our powerlessness, the shadows offer the secret of our power. This book is a history of the shadows, of the darkness in which hope lies. I want to start the history of this present moment over again, not with the election or the war but with a series of surprises from the shadows that ushered in this millennium.

6

The Millennium Arrives: November 9, 1989

I was born the summer the Berlin Wall went up, into a world shadowed by the Cold War between the United States and the USSR. Many people then expected a nuclear war was imminent and that such a war could mean the end of the world. People have always been good at imagining the end of the world, which is much easier to picture than the strange sidelong paths of change in a world without end. In the early sixties, international politics seemed deadlocked, but elsewhere things were stirring. The civil rights movement had already transformed the status quo into a crisis, not only for the officials dealing with demonstrators but for Americans whose conscience had woken up or whose patience had worn out.

That year Women's Strike for Peace was founded when a hundred thousand women in a hundred communities across the country staged a simultaneous one-day strike, launching an antinuclear peace movement that also prefigured the women's movement soon to be born. That year, Cesar Chavez was considering leaving his community organizer job to try to unionize California's farm workers, and the science writer Rachel Carson was finishing *Silent Spring*, her landmark denunciation of pesticides published in 1962. Just as the civil rights movement achieved not only specific gains but a change in the imagination of race and justice, so Carson's book was instrumental not only in getting DDT banned in the United States—which reversed the die-offs of many species of bird—but also in popularizing a worldview in which nature was made up not of inert objects but of interactive, interconnected systems, a worldview that would come to be called ecological. Step by step, ecological ideas have entered the mainstream to transform the imagination of the earth and its processes, of fire, water, air, soil, species, interdependences, biodiversities, watersheds, food chains (these latter words also entered the common vocabulary in recent times). In 1962, Students for a Democratic Society, the key organization for the student movement in the United States, was founded, and the environmental movement began to matter in public imagination and public discourse.

I was born into a world in which there was little or no recourse and often not even words for racial profiling, hate crimes, domestic violence, sexual harassment, homophobia, and other forms of exclusion and oppression. In my own country, which considered itself then as now a bastion of democracy, some of the Ivy League universities did not admit women, many of the Southern colleges and universities only admitted whites, and quite a few elite institutions still banned Jews. It was a world where the scope for decisions about religion, sexuality, living arrangements, food, and consumption patterns was far narrower, though there were also many old ways of life disappearing. Pristine wildernesses, family farms, small businesses, independent media, local customs, and indigenous practices were under siege by the homogenizations, consolidations, and commercializations that would supernova into corporate globalization, and the very premises from which to resist these eradications were still mostly embryonic. This is the way the world changes, as Dickens understood when he opened his most political novel with "It was the best of times, it was the worst of times." It usually is.

What gets called "the sixties" left a mixed legacy and a lot of divides. But it opened everything to question, and what seems most fundamental and most pervasive about all the ensuing changes is a loss of faith in authority: the authority of government, of patriarchy, of progress, of capitalism, of violence, of whiteness. The answers—the alternatives—haven't always been clear or easy, but the questions and the questioning are nevertheless significant. What's most important here is to feel the profundity of the changes, to feel how far we have come from that moment of Cold War summer. We inhabit, in ordinary daylight, a future that was unimaginably dark a few decades ago, when people found the end of the world easier to envision than the impending changes in everyday roles, thoughts, practices that not even the wildest science fiction anticipated. Perhaps we should not have adjusted to it so easily. It would be better if we were astonished every day.

I was born the summer the Berlin Wall went up, and I cried when I saw live footage of it coming down twenty-eight years later, on November 9, 1989. The massive wall had seemed eternal, like the Cold War itself, and the East Germans streaming across and the people celebrating in the streets were amazed, delighted, moved beyond imagining. East German authorities had given permission for orderly traffic across the wall, not for its eradication as a boundary altogether. It was because so many people showed up on both sides that the guards surrendered control altogether. People armed with nothing more than desire or hope brought down the wall. It was a year of miracles, if change wrought by determination against overwhelming odds can be a miracle and perhaps the greatest year of revolutions ever, greater than in 1848, far greater than in 1775 or 1789. In May the students of Tiananmen Square had mounted the first direct challenge to the authority of the Chinese government, and though they were defeated, they were only the first of a series of revolutions, or revelations. At the end of 1989,

Nelson Mandela was released from his South African prison after almost three decades behind bars.

Central Europe liberated itself that fall, one nation after another, Poland, East Germany, Hungary, Czechoslovakia (which later divided peacefully into the Czech Republic and Slovakia), using festively and bravely the nonviolent techniques wrought in other parts of the world. In the wake of the collapse of the Soviet Bloc, the Soviet Union collapsed too, or rather was dismantled by the will of the people and the guidance of the extraordinary president then, Mikhail Gorbachev, and his will to let go of power. The Soviet Union ceased to exist on Christmas of 1991. Some of the revolutions came about as the result of increasingly bold democratic organizing, notably that of the Solidarity Movement in Poland, where free elections were held that June after a decade of carefully laid groundwork. But others were more surprising, more spontaneous. The marches in the streets, the insistence of people upon exercising their rights as citizens, the sudden coming to voice of the voiceless, were central acts in a moment when a world order seemed at the edge of collapse. By acting as if they were free, the people of Eastern Europe became free.

Often the road to the future is through the past. Thus it was that in Hungary and Czechoslovakia marches commemorating political martyrs turned into nonviolent revolutions freeing the living. Often the road to politics is through culture. It was, for example, the 1976 persecution of the Czech band The Plastic People of the Universe that sparked Charter 77, the defiant manifesto issued on the New Year, some of whose signatories were key players in 1989. "It was not a bolt out of the blue, of course," wrote Charter signatory and playwright Vaclav Havel long before he became president of a postcommunist Czechoslovakia, "but that impression is understandable, since the ferment that led to it took place in the 'hidden sphere,' in that semi-darkness where things are difficult to chart or analyze. The chances of predicting the appearance of the Charter were just as slight as the chances are now of predicting where it will lead."

One could trace the equally strange trajectory that created rock and roll out of African and Scots-Irish musical traditions in the American South, then sent rock and roll around the world, so that a sound that had once been endemic to the South was intrinsic to dissent in Europe's east. Or the ricocheting trajectory by which Thoreau, abolitionists, Tolstoy, women suffragists, Gandhi, Martin Luther King Jr., and various others had over the course of more than a century wrought a doctrine of civil disobedience and nonviolence that would become standard liberatory equipment in every part of the world. If atomic bombs are the worst invention of the twentieth century, this practice might be the best, as well as the antithesis of those bombs. Or perhaps the music should be counted too. (That both the civil rights movement and rock-and-roll came out of the African American South to change the world suggests a startling, resistant richness under all that poverty and oppression and evokes, yet again, the strange workings of history.) The new era in which we're living did not come into being on the uneventful day of January 1, 2000 (or 2001, for those who are picky about calendric time). It came into being in stages, and is still being born, but each of these five dates—in 1989, 1994, 1999, 2001, 2003—constitutes a labor pang, an emergence out of emergency. The millennium was long anticipated as a moment of arrival, as the end of time, but it is instead a beginning of sorts, for something that is increasingly recognizable but yet unnamed, yet unrecognized, a new ground for hope.

7

The Millennium Arrives: January 1, 1994

O n New Year's Day of 1994, a guerrilla army of indigenous men, women, and children came from their homes in the Lacandon jungle and mountains of Chiapas, Mexico's southernmost state, and took the world by surprise and six towns by storm. In honor of Emiliano Zapata, another indigenous Mexican rebel at the other end of the twentieth century, they called themselves the Zapatistas and their philosophy Zapatismo. The fall of the Soviet Bloc was framed as the triumph of capitalism: capitalists increased their assertions that the "free market" was tantamount to democracy and freedom, and the 1990s would see the rise of neoliberalism. The Zapatistas chose to rise on the day that NAFTA, the North American Free Trade Agreement, went into effect, opening US, Mexican, and Canadian borders. The Zapatistas recognized what a decade has proved: NAFTA was an economic death sentence for hundreds of thousands of small-scale Mexican farmers and, with them, something of rural and traditional life.

In dazzling proclamations and manifestos, the Zapatistas announced the rise of the fourth world and the radical rejection of neoliberalism. They were never much of a military force, but their intellectual and imaginative power has been staggering. As radical historian and activist Elizabeth Martínez notes, "Zapatismo rejects the idea of a vanguard leading the people. Instead it is an affirmation of communal people's power, of grassroots autonomy . . . The Zapatistas say they are not proposing to take power but rather to contribute to a vast movement that would return power to civil society, using different forms of struggle." They came not just to enact a specific revolution but to bring a revolution, so to speak, in the nature of revolutions. They critiqued the dynamics of power, previous revolutions, capitalism, colonialism, militarism, sexism, racism, occasionally Marxism, recognizing the interplay of many forces and agendas in any act, any movement. They were nothing so simple as socialists, and they did not posit the old vision of state socialism as a solution to the problems of neoliberalism. They affirmed women's full and equal rights, refusing to be the revolution that sacrifices or postpones one kind of justice for another. They did not attempt to export their revolution but invited others to find their own local version of it, and from their forests and villages they entered into conversation with the world through *encuentros*, or encounters—conferences of a sort, communiqués, emissaries, and correspondence. For the rest of us, the Zapatistas came as a surprise and as a demonstration that overnight the most marginal, overlooked place can become the center of the world.

They were not just demanding change, but embodying it; and in this, they were and are already victorious. "Todo para todos, nada para nosotros" is one of their maxims—"Everything for everyone, nothing for ourselves," and though they have survived more than won their quarrel with the Mexican government, they have set loose glorious possibilities for activists everywhere. They understood the interplay between physical actions, those carried out with guns, and symbolic actions, those carried out with words, with images, with art, with communications, and they won through these latter means what they never could have won through their small capacity for violence. Some of their guns were only gun-shaped chunks of wood, as though the

Zapatistas were actors in a pageant, not soldiers in a war. This brilliantly enacted pageant caught the hearts and imaginations of Mexican civil society and activists around the world.

The Zapatistas came down from the mountains wearing bandannas and balaclavas, and though most of them were small of stature and dark-eyed, their spokesman was a tall, green-eyed intellectual who spoke several languages and smoked a pipe through the black balaclava he has never been seen without. Subcommandante Marcos, who came several years before 1994 to liberate the campesinos and was liberated from the conventionally leftist ideology with which he arrived, is the composer of a new kind of political discourse. For Marcos's is one of the great literary voices of our time, alternately allegorical, paradoxical, scathing, comic, and poetic, and his writings found their way around the world via a new medium, the Internet. His words express not his own ideas alone, exactly—after all he claims to be a subordinate, a subcommandante, and remains masked and pseudonymous—but those of a community bringing into being what those words propose. A singular voice that is a trumpet for a community, a writer composing a bridge across the gap between thoughts and acts.

Zapatista scholar and activist Manuel Callahan points out that the Zapatistas did not come to turn back the clock to some lost indigenous dreamtime but to hasten the arrival of the future: "We Indian peoples have come in order to wind the clock and to thus ensure that the inclusive, tolerant, and plural tomorrow which is, incidentally, the only tomorrow possible, will arrive," Marcos has said. "In order to do that, in order for our march to make the clock of humanity march, we Indian peoples have resorted to the art of reading what has not yet been written. Because that is the dream which animates us as indigenous, as Mexicans and, above all, as human beings. With our struggle, we are reading the future which has already been sown yesterday, which is being cultivated today, and which can only be reaped if one fights, if, that is, one dreams."

Elsewhere, in uncharacteristically straightforward terms, Marcos defined what the Zapatistas were not, if not exactly what they are, saying that if the army they initially appeared to be

> perpetuates itself as an armed military structure, it is headed for failure. Failure as an alternative set of ideas, an alternative attitude to the world. The worst that could happen to it, apart from that, would be to come to power and install itself as a revolutionary army. For us it would be a failure. What would be a success for the politico-military organizations of the sixties or seventies which emerged with the national liberation movements would be a fiasco for us. We have seen that such victories proved in the end to be failures, or defeats, hidden behind the mask of success. That what always remained unresolved was the role of people, of civil society, in what became ultimately a dispute between two hegemonies.

There is an amazing moment in George Orwell's *Homage to Catalonia*, his account of his participation in the Spanish Civil War and of the internal feuds between the anarchists and Communists that undermined their resistance to the Fascists, who won (with the help of Hitler and Mussolini, but not forever: Spain rushed back to democracy as soon as Franco died, in 1975). Orwell was too rigorously honest a man to toe any political line well; he was always noting the flaws in the ideologies—it was as though he was incapable of keeping his mind on a sufficient plane of abstraction, where ideology and rhetoric fly most freely. In his account of the trench warfare between the Fascists and the Loyalist anarchists, he wrote about the slogans the two sides shouted back and forth. The anarchists would shout out slogans, in Orwell's words, "full of revolutionary sentiments which explained to the Fascist soldiers that they were merely the hirelings of international capitalism, that they were fighting against their own class, etc., etc., and urged them to come over to our side . . . There is very little doubt it had its effect; everyone agreed that the trickle of Fascist deserters was partly caused by it."

Orwell says the man who did the main shouting on his side

was an artist at the job. Sometimes, instead of shouting revolutionary slogans he simply told the Fascists how much better we were fed than they were. His account of the Government rations was apt to be a little imaginative. "Buttered toast!"—you could hear his voice echoing across the lonely valley—"We're just sitting down to hot buttered toast over here! Lovely slices of buttered toast!" I do not doubt that, like the rest of us, he had not seen butter for weeks or months past, but in the icy night the news of buttered toast probably set many a Fascist mouth watering. It even made mine water, though I knew he was lying.

Those shouts about toast in the trenches prefigure the political speech of the current era, a playful language whose meaning is more than literal and whose spirit is more generous than ideology, an invitation rather than an order or a condemnation. You might say that the Spaniard yelling about toast wasn't lying, but composing, composing a literature of the trenches, transcending propaganda to make art. And I wonder if what he said was this: That the anarchists were more humane than the Fascists because they recognized that beneath the abstractions of political rhetoric are desires that are concrete, real, bodily, because they left room for improvisation and playfulness, pleasure and independence. The anarchic rhetoric of hot buttered toast is Marcos's language of evocation, description, parable and paradox, full of words that describe things—of birds, bread, blood, clouds—and of words of the heart, of love, dignity, and particularly hope. Its humor recognizes ironies, impossibilities and disproportions. It is the language of the vast nameless current movement that globalization has drawn together, a movement or movements driven by imaginations as supple as art rather than as stiff as dogma.

On January 1, 1996, the Fourth Declaration of the Lacandon Jungle was issued. It reads in part,

A new lie is being sold to us as history. The lie of the defeat of hope, the lie of the defeat of dignity, the lie of the defeat of humanity . . . In place of humanity, they offer us the stock market index. In place of dignity, they offer us the globalization of misery. In place of hope, they offer us emptiness. In place of life, they offer us an International of Terror. Against the International of Terror that neo-liberalism represents, we must raise an International of Hope. Unity, beyond borders, languages, colors, cultures, sexes, strategies and thoughts, of all those who prefer a living humanity. The International of Hope. Not the bureaucracy of hope, not an image inverse to, and thus similar to, what is annihilating us. Not power with a new sign or new clothes. A flower, yes, that flower of hope.

The Zapatista uprising was many kinds of revolution, was a green stone thrown in water whose ripples are still spreading outward, was a flower whose weightless seeds were taken up by the wind.

8

The Millennium Arrives:
November 30, 1999

As the end of the twentieth century approached, many people became preoccupied with the "Y2K problem"—with the theory that computers that had not been programmed to deal with four-digit year changes would somehow disable themselves at the stroke of midnight on 12/31/99, and the systems upon which we depend would crash. It was exemplary of a certain radical mindset, morbidity made attractive by anticipated vindication. It never came to pass, of course, but it was good for water and battery sales, and another kind of systemic crash came a month earlier.

I remember walking the streets of Seattle on November 30, 1999, thinking that the millennium was already here, feeling that enormous exhilaration of consciously living in history. For all around, in intersection after intersection of the gridded, gritty old downtown, people had blockaded the World Trade Organization (WTO) meeting. There were union and agricultural and human rights activists, environmentalists, anarchists, religious groups, students, and grandparents. The WTO had been founded to control international trade and, more importantly, to suppress or outlaw all other powers to limit and manage this trade. Though those who oppose it are sometimes called "globophobes" or "antiglobalization" activists, the term *globalization* can apply to many kinds of internationalization and border-crossing, and what we oppose is more accurately corporate globalization and its ideology, neoliberalism, or sometimes capitalism altogether. Thus, the movement is now sometimes called anticapitalism, though it is more complex, is for more things, and is less like classical Marxism or socialism than that term suggests—I like the term *global justice movement* for this swarm of resistances and inspirations. Another way to boil down the essential principles would focus on the privatizations and consolidations of power corporate globalization represents and see the resistance to it as, simply, a struggle to re-democratize the world, or the corner of it from which a given struggle is mounted.

After all, this form of globalization would essentially suspend local, regional, and national rights of self-determination over labor, environmental, and agricultural conditions in the name of the dubious benefits of the free market, benefits that would be enforced by unaccountable transnational authorities acting primarily to protect the rights of capital. At a recent labor forum, Dave Bevard, a laid-off US union metalworker, referred to this new world order as "government of the corporations, by the corporations, for the corporations." Much of what free trade has brought about is what gets called "the race to the bottom," the quest for the cheapest possible wages or agricultural production, with consequent losses on countless fronts. The argument is always that such moves make industry more profitable, but it would be more accurate to say that free trade concentrates profit away from workers and communities, for whom it is therefore far less profitable (and here the very term *profit* cries out for redefinition, for the stock market defines as profitable every kind of destruction and lacks terms for valuing cultures, diversities, or long-term wellbeing, let alone happiness, beauty, freedom, or justice).

The corporate agenda of NAFTA and related globalization treaties is demonstrated most famously by the case of MTBE, a gasoline additive that causes severe damage to human health and the environment. When California banned it, the Canadian corporation Methanex filed a lawsuit demanding nearly a billion dollars in compensation from the US government for profit lost because of the ban. Under NAFTA rules, corporations have an absolute right to profit with which local laws must not interfere. Poisoning the well is no longer a crime, but stopping the free flow of poison meets with punishment. Other examples of this kind of globalization include the attempts by multinational corporations to privatize water supplies and to patent genes, including the genes of wild and of traditionally cultivated plants—to lock up as commodities much of the basic stuff of life, in the name of free trade.

Young global justice advocates understand that, as is often said, globalization is war by other means. War is easy to abhor, but it takes a serious passion to unravel the tangles of financial manipulations and to understand the pain of sweatshop workers or displaced farmers. And maybe this is what heroism looks like nowadays: occasionally high-profile heroism in public but mostly just painstaking mastery of arcane policy, stubborn perseverance year after year for a cause, empathy with those who remain unseen, and outrage channeled into dedication. There had been opposition to corporate globalization before, most notably the Zapatista uprising on the day that NAFTA went into effect. But Seattle gathered the growing momentum and made it impossible to ignore.

Economic historian Charles Derber writes,

> The excitement of Seattle was the subliminal sense that a new opposition, and perhaps a whole new kind of politics, was being born, both in the United States and the world at large . . . Seattle was mainly a group of white folks. Yet, and this was very important, there were people from India, Mexico, the Philippines, and Indonesia. They represented influential groups and millions of

people who had protested on their own streets but couldn't come to Seattle. So if one looks at the larger movement and the swelling of the ranks of globalization activists around the world, one would have to conclude that this is truly a crossnational movement and very possibly the first truly global movement.

French farmer and revolutionary Jose Bové, who was also there, had a similar response: "I had the feeling that a new period of protest was about to begin in America—a new beginning for politics, after the failures and inactivities of the previous generation."

The global justice movement brought to the progressive/radical community what had long been missing: a comprehensive analysis that laid the groundwork for a broad coalition, for the common ground so absent from the movements of the 1970s and 1980s, which seemed to advance a single sector or pit one issue against another. This is, of course, in part because the globalizing corporations manage to be anti-environmental, antidemocratic, and a whole lot of other atrocities all at once. But the antiglobalization movement in its breadth, in its flexibility and its creativity seems, like the Zapatistas, a great step toward reinventing revolution. The year the Zapatistas stepped onto the world stage, the radical geographer Iain Boal had prophesied, "The longing for a better world will need to arise at the imagined meeting place of many movements of resistance, as many as there are sites of closure and exclusion. The resistance will be as transnational as capitalism." That resistance had appeared before Seattle, as Reclaim the Streets and the antiroads movement in Britain, as anti-GMO activism in France and India, as indigenous rights movements in Latin America, but it was in that upper left corner of the United States that it made its transnational presence impossible to ignore.

Fifty thousand people joined the union-led march, and ten thousand activists blockaded in the downtown streets, disrupting and ultimately canceling the meeting of the WTO that day. The shutdown encouraged impoverished-nation delegates and the representatives of nongovernmental organizations to stand their ground inside the WTO talks. This time victory—the shutdown—was tangible and immediate. But the action also served to galvanize the world with an unanticipated revolt on the grand scale, and it made corporate globalization a subject of debate as it had not been before.

In Seattle on those two days, there were police riots, police brutality, injuries, hospitalizations, and arrests in violation of First Amendment rights. The famous solidarity—"teamsters and turtles" for the union members and the sea turtle–costumed environmentalists—did not preclude alienation and infighting. Seattle is sometimes misremembered as an Eden. It was just a miracle, a messy one that won't happen the same way again. Since the Seattle surprise, it's become standard practice to erect a miniature police state of walls and weapons around any globalization summit, and these rights-free zones seem to prefigure what corporation globalization promises.

But at the end of November 1999, the media, which had dozed through the massive antinuclear, antiwar, and environmental actions of the eighties and nineties, woke up with a start to proclaim this shutdown the biggest thing since the sixties. In a way it was, in part because they made it so, in part because it was the next phase built upon the failures and successes of previous eras. In Seattle, the tactics and philosophy of nonviolent direct action had a shining moment, a moment that was the culmination of decades of discussion and experimentation. In the introduction to his anthology *The Battle of Seattle*, Eddie Yuen writes of the two principles behind this kind of action:

> The first of these is the adoption of a strict nonviolence code that was a response to a macho fascination with revolutionary violence in the '60s. The second is the commitment to direct democracy, as specifically the organizational forms of the affinity group, decentralized spokes-council meetings and consensus process. This commitment was a response to the preponderance of charismatic (and almost always male) leadership cults as well as the increasingly authoritarian organizational forms that became popular during the late New Left.

That is to say, the movement was pluralist; it came from many directions, including a constructive critique of the failures of the 1960s and an ethics of power. So you could say that Seattle arose not only from addressing the problem that is "them"—the corporations and governments—but from the problems that have often been "us," the activists, the radicals, the revolution. Its success came out of addressing both of these fronts, a response many years in the making. And out of the moment.

Perhaps you've forgotten that in 1999 the arrogance of the boom years was still upon us; corporate chief executive officers were treated like rock stars; business journalists babbled that the market could go up forever without going down. Then the technology bubble burst; the Enron and WorldCom scandals broke, demonstrating that the corporations were morally bankrupt too; Argentina went bust thanks to its adherence to neoliberal fiscal policies, ran though several governments, defaulted on its loans and remains today a place of great economic crisis and greater anarchic social innovation. A decade after communism collapsed, capitalism was a wreck. And now, five years after Seattle, the WTO, which before that November day looked like an inexorable tank, ready to crush anything in its path, is still a tank, but one stuck in a ditch.

On that day when Seattle seemed like the center of the world, there was a sister action in Bangalore, India, focusing on Monsanto, which once brought the world the defoliant Agent Orange and, more recently, has been bringing it a cornucopia of genetically modified crops whose main features seem to be resistance to Monsanto pesticides and enhancement of Monsanto profits. The corporation that so embodied the WTO's threats has in recent years closed its European office, been widely attacked in India, given up altogether on marketing its GMO wheat, taken its New Leaf potato out of production after the market for it collapsed, stopped trying to spread GMO canola in Australia, been unable to collect royalties on GMO soybeans grown in South America, and reported record losses in 2004. Citizens in Italy turned 13 of its 20 regions and 1,500 towns into "GMO-free zones," as did citizens in several California counties. The huge corporation Syngenta also canceled all its research and marketing programs for GMO products in Europe because of popular outcry. European citizens have achieved significant successes in limiting the reach of GMO foods and agriculture into that continent, despite the lack of opposition (or, thanks to the WTO, inability to mount opposition) of their national governments.

To think of 1999 is to think of a bygone era in which these more complex and long-term issues had not been overshadowed by the imperial belligerence of the so-called War on Terror. But it is also to think of a great turning point, the moment a powerful movement against corporate globalization had coalesced. Four years later a group led by Mexican *campesinos* and Korean farmers, in coalition with the NGOs inside the September 2003 WTO ministerial in Cancun, brought the organization to the brink of collapse.

Before it began we expected that the talks would falter. The United States and the EU were pressuring the impoverished countries to surrender more autonomy without giving them any reward and without being willing to address the way agricultural subsidies in the developed world ravage farming in the less developed one. But thanks to an unanticipated solidarity among activists, nongovernmental organizations, and impoverished nations, the WTO talks didn't just falter; they collapsed spectacularly. An activist e-mailed us from the frontlines, "A woman from Swaziland turned to a colleague of mine and told him that the African countries could not have stood firm against the WTO, the US, and the EU if it had not been for the activists in and outside of the convention hall. She said that our actions in and outside, our words, our pressure—particularly as they reached the press—gave her and her fellow African nations the strength to take this historic stand." Another activist says that it was the presence of the farmers outside that pressured the nations inside to stand up, to remember whose lives were at stake, that kept Korea, for example, where one out of six families farms, from bargaining away more of its local agriculture. At the Cancun ministerial, the impoverished nations created a coalition called the Group of Twenty-Plus that represents nearly half the world's people and more than two-thirds of its farmers, a group powerful enough to stand up to the rich nations and the corporations they represent. The coalition (in which India, China, and many smaller nations didn't have to reconcile their differences) was assembled by Brazil, which under the leadership of Luiz Inácio "Lula" da Silva is a beautiful maverick. This is one of the global impacts of South America's long climb out of tyranny. At 3 p.m. on the last day of the meeting, the Kenyan delegate said, "This meeting is over. This is another Seattle," and with that the Group of Twenty-Plus walked and the talks collapsed. The nongovernmental organization members present went wild with joy and the demonstrators outside began to celebrate. *Guardian* commentator George Monbiot wrote, "At Cancun the weak nations stood up to the most powerful negotiators on earth and were not broken. The lesson they will bring home is that if this is possible, almost anything is."

It was a triumph for farmers, for the poor, for the power of nonviolent direct action, for the power of people over corporations and justice over greed. It was a power shift, both from the rich nations to the poor and from the towers to the streets. Seattle was led by young white radicals, though representatives of all the world were there, but Cancun was led by Mexican *campesinos* and Korean farmers representing huge constituencies (including seventy nations and the hundred million members of the groups in the Via Campesino coalition), which gave it a different tone and a different authority. They were able to speak for the world as we were not. And they demonstrated how broad-based the movement was, how meaningful the common ground attained by such different players. Unfolding as it did on the second anniversary of 9/11, the revolution in Cancun reclaimed some of the peaceful populist power that Osama bin Laden and Bush had paralyzed.

"We are winning," said the graffiti in Seattle.

9

The Millennium Arrives: September 11, 2001

The airplanes that became bombs were from any perspective a terrible thing. But there was a moment when something beautiful might have come out of it, not only the heroism of those on site but of those across the country. A President Gore, a President Nader would not have been adequate to the moment. To imagine a leader who could have risen to the occasion, you'd have to reach further, to a President Winona LaDuke (the half-Jewish, half-indigenous environmentalist who was the Green Party candidate for vice president in 2000) or to a parallel universe with a President Martin Luther King. Of course there were belligerent and racist and jingoistic reactions, but there was a long moment when almost everyone seemed to pause, an opening when the nation might have taken another path. And some took that path anyway. In the hours and days that followed everyone agreed that the world was changed, though no one knew exactly how. It was not just the possibility of a war but the sense of the relation between self and world that changed, at least for Americans.

To live entirely for oneself in private is a huge luxury, a luxury countless aspects of this society encourage, but like a diet of pure foie gras it clogs and narrows the arteries of the heart. This is what we're encouraged to crave in this country, but most of us crave more deeply something with more grit, more substance. Since my home county was faced with a disastrous drought when I was fifteen, I have been fascinated by the way people rise to the occasion of a disaster. In that drought, the wealthy citizens of that county enjoyed self-denial for the public good more than they enjoyed private abundance the rest of the time. The 1989 Loma Prieta quake shook San Francisco into the here and now: I remember how my anger at someone suddenly ceased to matter, and so did my plans. The day after the quake, I walked around town to see people I cared about, and the world was local and immediate. Not just because the Bay Bridge was damaged and there were practical reasons to stay home, but because the long-term perspective from which so much dissatisfaction and desire comes was shaken too: life, meaning, value were close to home, in the present. We who had been through the quake were present and connected. Connected to death, to fear, to the unknown, but in being so connected one could feel empathy, passion, and heroism as well. We could feel strongly, and that is itself something hard to find in the anesthetizing distractions of this society.

That first impulse everywhere on September 11 was to give blood, a kind of secular communion in which people offered up the life of their bodies for strangers. The media dropped its advertisements, leers, and gossip and told us about tragedy and heroism. Giving blood and volunteering were the first expression of a sense of connection; the flag became an ambiguous symbol of that connection, since it meant everything from empathy to belligerence. In Brooklyn that week, a friend reported, "Nobody went to work and everybody talked to strangers." What makes people heroic and what makes them feel members of a community? I hoped that one thing to come out of the end of American invulnerability would be a stronger sense of what disasters abroad—massacres, occupations, wars, famines, dictatorships—mean and feel like, a sense of citizenship in the world.

There were spectacular heroes in this disaster, the firefighters, police, and medical and sanitation workers who did what could be done at the site afterward and those who died trying in those first hours. But I mean *heroism* as a comparatively selfless state of being and as a willingness to do. Wartime and disaster elicit this heroism most strongly, though there are always volunteers who don't wait until disaster comes home, the volunteers and activists who engage with issues that don't affect them directly, with landmines, discrimination, genocide, the people who want to extend their own privilege and security to those who lack them. In its mildest form that heroism is simply citizenship, a sense of connection and commitment to the community, and for a few months after 9/11 we had a strange surge of citizenship in this country.

Shortly after the bombing, the president swore to "eliminate evil" from the world, and with this he seemed to promise that the goodness that filled us would not be necessary in the future, a future in which we could return to preoccupation with our private lives. Though oil politics had much to do with what had happened, we were not asked to give up driving or vehicles that gulp huge amounts of fuel; we were asked to go shopping and to spy on our neighbors.

It seemed as though the Bush administration recognized this extraordinary possibility of the moment and did everything it could to suppress it, for nothing is more dangerous to them than that sense of citizenship, fearlessness, and communion with the world that is distinct from the blind patriotism driven by fear. They used 9/11 as an excuse to launch attacks inside and outside the United States, but it was not an inevitable or even a legitimate response—in fact, 9/11 was largely an excuse to carry out existing agendas of imperial expansion and domestic repression. Bush the First had neglected the chances the end of the Cold War gave us, and his son made the worst of the invitations this new emergency offered. I wish 9/11 had not happened, but I wish the reaction that hovered on the brink of being born had.

10

The Millennium Arrives: February 15, 2003

O r perhaps that moment did come seventeen months later, when we marched against the Iraq War on all the continents of the earth, a *we* that is the antithesis of Bush's post-9/11 proclamation that "You're either with us or against us." Organized via the Internet without leaders or a single ideology, this unprecedented global wave of protest demonstrated the decentralizing political power of that medium, and like Seattle it countered the Internet's disembodied placelessness with bodies come together in thousands of cities and in places that weren't urban at all. A march is when bodies speak by walking, when private citizens become that mystery the public, when traversing the boulevards of cities becomes a way to travel toward political goals. It answered that moment of murder and division on 9/11 with a moment of communion around the world, a moment of trust between the strangers who marched together, a moment when history would be made not by weapons and secrets but walkers under the open sky. What was most remarkable about the huge peace marches in San Francisco was the sense of ebullience and exhilaration, as though people had finally found something they'd long craved—a chance to speak out, to participate, to see that others shared their beliefs, to be saying these things someplace where it might matter rather than murmuring about them in private. It was moving and disconcerting to realize that these experiences—the experience of democracy and of citizenship—were so unusual and so desired. Most of the tens of thousands of signs were homemade, and most were beautiful or funny or scathing. Each of the signs was simple in itself but by the thousand they constituted a sophisticated marshaling of all the arguments against a war against Iraq. I saw a group of Palestinian women on the north side of the street, demure in wool challis headscarves, and directly across from them but screened off by the hordes who streamed by were two young women, one white, one Asian, holding signs depicting your basic scribbled female pubic triangle, inscribed "This Bush for Peace." There was, it seemed, room for everyone.

Periodically a huge roar would go up from the crowd, a roar with no cause I could ever locate, as though the mass of people had become one huge beast reveling in a power that was not violence but strength. With between eleven and thirty million participants around the globe, it was the biggest and most widespread collective protest the world has ever seen, and if you count the small demonstration at MacMurdo Station in Antarctica, the first to reach all seven continents. As Archbishop Desmond Tutu pointed out from Manhattan, it was unprecedented to have such broad action against a war that had yet to begin. And there, in Manhattan, where the World Trade Towers had collapsed seventeen months before, more than four hundred thousand people gathered illegally—no march permit was ever issued, yet they gathered anyway—to refuse to endorse the revenge being exacted for that crime (for those who credulously believed that Iraq was somehow linked to al-Qaeda). The *New York Times* described popular protest as the world's other superpower. 9/11 had been a moment of communion born out of atrocity, but this one was born out of insurgency and outraged idealism. It bore witness to a usually unspoken desire for something other than ordinary private life, for something more risky, more involved, more idealistic. Perhaps many or most are not really ready to live up to that desire, but it is there, an aquifer of pure passion.

At an event that March, Robert Muller, a peace activist and former assistant secretary general of the United Nations, astounded an audience anticipating war with his optimism. He exclaimed, "I'm so honored to be alive at such a miraculous time in history. I'm so moved by what's going on in our world today. Never before in the history of the world has there been a global, visible, public, viable, open dialogue and conversation about the very legitimacy of war." Journalist Lynne Twist reports that he added, "All of this is taking place in the context of the United Nations Security Council, the body that was established in 1949 for exactly this purpose. He pointed out that it has taken us more than fifty years to realize that function, the real function of the UN . . . Dr. Muller was almost in tears in recognition of the fulfillment of this dream."

The dream did not last, though the moment is worth cherishing. Instead came the nightmare of burned and maimed children, bombed civilians, soldiers incinerated by depleted-uranium rounds, history itself wiped out when the United States permitted the looting of Baghdad's National Museum and the burning of its National Library, US soldiers picked off a few at a time during the months of occupation and insurrection. The millions marching on February 15 represented something that is not yet fully realized, an extraordinary potential waiting, waiting for some catalyst to bring it into full flower. A new imagination of politics and change is already here, and I want to try to pare away what obscures it.

11

Changing the Imagination of Change

A lot of activists seem to have a mechanistic view of change, or perhaps they expect what quack diet pills offer, "Quick and easy results guaranteed." They expect finality, definitiveness, straightforward cause-and-effect relationships, instant returns, and as a result they specialize in disappointment, which sinks in as bitterness, cynicism, defeatism, knowingness. They operate on the premise that for every action there is an equal and opposite and punctual reaction and regard the lack of one as failure. After all, we are often a reaction: Bush decides to invade Iraq; we create a global peace movement. Sometimes success looks instant: we go to Seattle and shut down the WTO, but getting to Seattle can be told as a story of months of organizing or decades of developing a movement smart enough and broad enough to understand the complex issues at hand and bring in the ten thousand who would blockade. History is made out of common dreams, groundswells, turning points, watersheds—it's a landscape more complicated than commensurate cause and effect, and that peace movement came out of causes with roots reaching far beyond and long before Bush.

Effects are not proportionate to causes—not only because huge causes sometimes seem to have little effect, but because tiny ones occasionally have huge consequences. Gandhi said, "First they ignore you. Then they laugh at you. Then they fight you. Then you win." But those stages unfold slowly. And as the law of unexpected activist consequences might lead you to expect, the abolition movement also sparked the first widespread women's rights movement, which took about the same amount of time to secure the right to vote for American women, has achieved far more in the subsequent eighty-four years, and is by no means done. Activism is not a journey to the corner store, it is a plunge into the unknown. The future is always dark.

Some years ago, scientists attempted to create a long-range weather forecasting program. It turned out that the most minute variations, even the undetectable things, the things they could perhaps not even yet imagine as data, could cause entirely different weather to emerge from almost identical initial conditions. This was famously summed up as the saying about the flap of a butterfly's wings on one continent that can change the weather on another. History is like weather, not like checkers. (And you, if you're lucky and seize the day, are like that butterfly.) Like weather in its complexity, in its shifts, in the way something triggers its opposite, just as a heat wave sucks the fog off the ocean and makes my town gray and clammy after a few days of baking, weather in its moods, in its slowness, in its suddenness.

A game of checkers ends. The weather never does. That's why you can't save anything. *Saving* is the wrong word, one invoked over and over again, for almost every cause. Jesus saves and so do banks: they set things aside from the flux of earthly change. We never did save the whales, though we might have prevented them from becoming extinct. We will have to continue to prevent that as long as they continue not to be extinct, unless we become extinct first. That might indeed save the whales, until the sun supernovas or the species evolves into something other than whales. *Saving* suggests a laying up where neither moth nor rust doth corrupt; it imagines an extraction from the dangerous, unstable, ever-changing process called life on earth. But life is never so tidy and final. Only death is. Environmentalists like to say that defeats are permanent, victories temporary. Extinction, like death, is forever, but protection needs to be maintained. But now, in a world where restoration ecology is becoming increasingly important, it turns out that even defeats aren't always permanent. Across the United States and Europe, dams have been removed, wetlands and rivers restored, once-vanished native species reintroduced, endangered species regenerated.

Americans are good at responding to a crisis and then going home to let another crisis brew both because we imagine that the finality of death can be achieved in life—it's called *happily ever after* in personal life, *saved* in politics and religion—and because we tend to think of political engagement as something for emergencies rather than, as people in many other countries (and Americans at other times) have imagined it, as a part and even a pleasure of everyday life. The problem seldom goes home. Most nations agree to a ban on hunting endangered species of whale, but their ocean habitat is compromised in other ways, such as fisheries depletion and contamination. DDT is banned in the United States but exported to the developing world, and its creator, the Monsanto corporation, moves on to the next experiment.

Going home seems to be a way to abandon victories when they're still delicate, still in need of protection and encouragement. Human babies are helpless at birth, and so perhaps are victories before they've been consolidated into the culture's sense of how things should be. I wonder sometimes what would happen if victory was imagined not just as the elimination of evil but the establishment of good—if, after American slavery had been abolished, Reconstruction's promises of economic justice had been enforced by the abolitionists, or if the end of apartheid had, similarly, been seen as meaning instituting economic justice as well (or, as some South Africans put it, ending economic apartheid).

It's always too soon to go home. Most of the great victories continue to unfold, unfinished in the sense that they are not yet fully realized, but also in the sense that they continue to spread influence. A phenomenon like the civil rights movement creates a vocabulary and a toolbox for social change used around the globe, so that its effects far outstrips its goals and specific achievements—and failures. Domestically, conservatives are still fighting and co-opting it, further evidence it's still potent. The left likes to lash itself for its reactive politics, but on many fronts—reproductive rights, affirmative action—it's the right that reacts, not always successfully.

How do you map the US Supreme Court's 2003 ruling that struck down the last of the laws criminalizing gay and lesbian sex? The conventional narrative would have it that the power rests in the hands of the nine robed ones; a more radical model would mention the gay Texas couple who chose to turn their lives inside out over many years to press the lawsuit; but a sort of cultural ecology would measure what made the nation rethink its homophobia, creating the societal change that the Supreme Court only assented to: they all count. It now looks likely that the Los Angeles River—that long concrete ditch through the city—will be restored over the next few dozen years, thanks to the stubborn visionaries who believe that even there a river could come back to life, and to the changing understanding of nature that has reached even administrators and engineers. We are not who we were not very long ago.

12

On the Indirectness
of Direct Action

A friend, Jaime Cortez, tells me I should consider the difference between hope and faith. Hope, he says, can be based on the evidence, on the track record of what might be possible—and in this book I've been trying to shift what the track record might be. But faith endures even when there's no way to imagine winning in the foreseeable future; faith is more mystical. Jaime sees the American left as pretty devoid of faith and connects faith to what it takes to change things in the long term, beyond what you might live to see or benefit from. I argue that what was once the left is now so full of anomalies—of indigenous intellectuals and Catholic pacifists and the like—that maybe we have faith, some of us.

Activism isn't reliable. It isn't fast. It isn't direct either, most of the time, even though the term *direct action* is used for that confrontation in the streets, those encounters involving lawbreaking and civil disobedience. It may be because activists move like armies through the streets that people imagine effects as direct as armies, but an army assaults the physical world and takes physical possession of it; activists reclaim the streets and occasionally seize a Bastille or topple a Berlin

Wall, but the terrain of their action is usually immaterial, the realm of the symbolic, political discourse, collective imagination. They enter the conversation forcefully, but it remains a conversation. Every act is an act of faith, because you don't know what will happen. You just hope and employ whatever wisdom and experience seems most likely to get you there.

I believe all this because I've lived it, and I've lived it because I'm a writer. For twenty years I have sat alone at a desk tinkering with sentences and then sending them out, and for most of my literary life the difference between throwing something in the trash and publishing it was imperceptible, but in the past several years the work has started coming back to me, or the readers have. Musicians and dancers face their audience and visual artists can spy on them, but reading is mostly as private as writing. Writing is lonely, it's an intimate talk with the dead, with the unborn, with the absent, with strangers, with the readers who may never come to be and who even if they read you will do so weeks, years, decades later. An essay, a book, is one statement in a long conversation you could call culture or history; you are answering something or questioning something that may have fallen silent long ago, and the response to your words may come long after you're gone and never reach your ears, if anyone hears you in the first place.

After all, this is how it's been for so many books that count, books that didn't shake the world when they first appeared but blossomed later. This is a model for how indirect effect can be, how delayed, how invisible; no one is more hopeful than a writer, no one is a bigger gambler. Thoreau's 1849 essay "Civil Disobedience" finally found its readers in the twentieth century when it was put into practice as part of the movements that changed the world (Thoreau's voice was little heard in his time, but it echoed across the continent in the 1960s and has not left us since. Emily Dickinson, Walt Whitman, Walter Benjamin, and Arthur Rimbaud, like Thoreau, achieved their greatest impact long after their deaths, long after weeds had grown over the graves of most of the bestsellers of their lifetimes.)

You write your books. You scatter your seeds. Rats might eat them, or they might rot. In California, some seeds lie dormant for decades because they only germinate after fire, and sometimes the burned landscape blooms most lavishly. In her book *Faith*, Sharon Salzberg recounts how she put together a collection of teachings by the Buddhist monk U Pandita and consigned the project to the "minor-good-deed category." Long afterward, she found out that while Aung San Suu Kyi, the Burmese democracy movement's leader, was isolated under house arrest by that country's dictators, the book and its instructions in meditation "became her main source of spiritual support during those intensely difficult years." Thought becomes action becomes the order of things, but no straight road takes you there.

Nobody can know the full consequences of their actions, and history is full of small acts that changed the world in surprising ways. I was one of thousands of activists at the Nevada Test Site in the late 1980s, an important, forgotten history still unfolding out there where the United States and Great Britain have exploded more than a thousand nuclear bombs with disastrous effects on the environment and human health (and where the Bush administration would like to resume testing, thereby tearing up the last shreds of the unratified Comprehensive Test Ban Treaty). Some of the largest acts of civil disobedience in American history were committed when we would walk into the place to be arrested as trespassers, thousands in a day. There too, as in peace marches, just walking became a form of political speech, one whose directness was a delight after all the usual avenues of politicking: sitting in front of computers, going to meetings, making phone calls, dealing with money. Among the throng arrested were Quakers, Buddhists, Shoshone, Mormons, pagans, anarchists, veterans, and physicists. We would barely make the news in the United States. But we were visible on the other side of the world.

Our acts inspired the Kazakh poet Olzhas Suleimenov on February 27, 1989, to read a manifesto instead of poetry on live Kazakh TV, a manifesto demanding a shutdown of the Soviet test site in Semipalatinsk, Kazakhstan, and to call a meeting. Five thousand Kazakhs gathered at the writers' union the next day and formed a movement that shut down the nuclear test site. They named themselves the Nevada-Semipalatinsk Antinuclear Movement, and they acted in concert with us. *Us* by that time included the Western Shoshone who had come to endorse our actions and point out that we and the United States government were on their land; the Kazakhs identified with these indigenous people.

Anyway, the Soviet test site was shut down. The catalyst was Suleimenov, and though we in Nevada were his inspiration, what gave him his platform was his poetry in a country that loves poets. There's a wonderful parable by Jorge Luis Borges. In the last years of the thirteenth century, God tells a leopard in a cage, "You live and will die in this prison so that a man I know of may see you a certain number of times and not forget you and place your figure and symbol in a poem which has its precise place in the scheme of the universe. You suffer captivity, but you will have given a word to the poem." The poem is the *Divine Comedy*; the man who sees the leopard is Dante. Perhaps Suleimenov wrote all his poems so that one day he could stand up in front of a TV camera and deliver not a poem but a manifesto. And Arundhati Roy wrote a ravishing novel, *The God of Small Things*, that catapulted her to international stardom, perhaps so that when she stood up to oppose dams and corporations and corruption and the destruction of the local, people would notice.

Or perhaps they opposed the ravaging of the earth so that poetry too would survive in the world. A couple of years ago, a friend wrote me to urge me to focus on the lyrical end of my writing rather than activism and I wrote back, "What is the purpose of resisting corporate globalization if not to protect the obscure, the ineffable, the unmarketable, the unmanageable, the local, the poetic, and the eccentric? So they need to be practiced, celebrated, and studied too, right now." I could have added that these acts themselves become forms of resistance; the two are not necessarily separate practices. All those years that I went to the Nevada Test Site to oppose nuclear testing, the experience was also about camping in the desert, about the beauty of the light and the grandeur of the space, about friendship and discovery. The place gave me far more than I could ever give it. Resistance is usually portrayed as a duty, but it can be a pleasure, an education, a revelation.

The year after the birth of the Nevada-Semipalatinsk Antinuclear Movement, when some of its members were already with us at the peace camp next to the Nevada Test Site, I was the only one who attended a workshop there on Nevada and the military. The man giving it was visibly disappointed but gave it splendidly for me alone. As we sat in the rocks and dust and creosote bush of the deep desert on a sunny day, the great Nevada organizer Bob Fulkerson taught me that the atrocities of nuclear testing were not unique in that state with a fifth of all the military land in the country and invited me to travel into its remote reaches. He is still a cherished friend of mine and still the executive director of a coalition he founded a few years later, the Progressive Leadership Alliance of Nevada (PLAN), the most potent statewide group of its kind, bringing together environmental, labor, and human rights groups.

What came of Bob's invitation changed my life and had much to do with my book *Savage Dreams*, the first half of which is about the Test Site and the strands of its history wrapped around the world, and before there was the book there was an essay version of what the Test Site and Bob taught me that appeared in a magazine with circulation of about half a million. A few years ago I went back to the Test Site for another spring action, and there I met several students from Evergreen College in Washington who had decided to come down because they had been reading *Savage Dreams* in class. If you're lucky, you carry a torch into that dark of Virginia Woolf's, and if you're really lucky you'll sometimes see to whom you've passed it, as I did on that day (and if you're polite, you'll remember who handed it to you). I don't know if the Evergreen kids have become great activists or died in a car crash on the way home, but I know that for them I was a leopard prompting a word or two of the poem of their own lives, as Bob was for me. Borges's parable continues. On his deathbed, Dante is told by God what the secret purpose of his life and work was. "Dante, in wonderment, knew at last who and what he was and blessed the bitterness of his life."

One day in Auschwitz, the writer Primo Levi recited a canto of Dante's *Inferno* to a companion, and the poem about hell reached out from six hundred years before to roll back Levi's despair and his dehumanization. It was the canto about Ulysses, and though it ends tragically, it contains the lines "You were not made to live like animals/But to pursue virtue and know the world," which he recited and translated to the man walking with him. Levi lived, and wrote marvelous books of his own, poetry after Auschwitz in the most literal sense.

In 1940, in his last letter to a friend before his death, the incomparable, uncategorizable German-Jewish essayist and theorist Walter Benjamin wrote, "Every line we succeed in publishing today—no matter how uncertain the future to which we entrust it—is a victory wrenched from the powers of darkness."

13

The Angel
of Alternate History

Benjamin wasn't always so optimistic. In the most celebrated passage of his "Theses on the Philosophy of History," he writes,

> This is how one pictures the angel of history. His face is turned
> toward the past. Where we perceive a chain of events, he sees one
> single catastrophe which keeps piling wreckage upon wreckage
> and hurls it in front of his feet. The angel would like to stay, awak-
> en the dead, and make whole what has been smashed, but a storm
> is blowing from Paradise; it has got caught in his wings with such
> violence that the angel can no longer close them.

History, in Benjamin's version, is a being to whom things happen, a creature whose despairing lineaments are only redeemed by the sublimity of the imagery. It's not hard to imagine why Benjamin would picture a tragic, immobilized history, for the storm of the Third Reich was upon him when he wrote his "Theses," and it would destroy him later that year. And tragedy is seductive. After all, it is beautiful. Survival is funny. It's the former that makes the greatest art. But I want to propose another angel, a comic angel, the Angel of Alternate History.

For several years I served on the board of Nevada's statewide non-profit environmental and antinuclear group, Citizen Alert (another consequence of meeting Bob Fulkerson). I wrote a fundraiser for it once, modeled after *It's a Wonderful Life*. The angel in that movie, who has the pointedly unheroic name Clarence, is hapless but not paralyzed, hopeful and bumbling. Director Frank Capra's movie is a model for radical history because Clarence shows the hero what the world would look like if he hadn't been there, the only sure way to measure the effect of our acts, the one we never get. The angel Clarence's face is turned toward the futures that never come to pass. In my fundraising letter, I described what Nevada might look like without this organization fighting the Yucca Mountain nuclear waste dump and various other atrocities visited upon the state by developers and the Departments of Defense and Energy. After all, most environmental victories look like nothing happened; the land wasn't annexed by the army, the mine didn't open, the road didn't cut through, the factory didn't spew effluents that didn't give asthma to the children who didn't wheeze and panic and stay indoors on beautiful days. They are triumphs invisible except through storytelling. Citizen Alert's biggest victory is almost forgotten: the cancellation in the 1980s of the MX missile program that would've turned eastern Nevada and western Utah into a giant sacrifice area to soak up the Soviet missiles in an all-out nuclear war (and pave over pristine desert to make the tracks the missiles would travel on).

Benjamin's angel tells us history is what happens, but the Angel of Alternate History tells that our acts count, that we are making history all the time, because of what doesn't happen as well as what does. Only that angel can see the atrocities not unfolding, but we could learn to study effects more closely. Instead we don't look, and a radical change too soon becomes status quo. Young women often don't know that sexual harassment and date rape are new categories; most forget how much more toxic rivers like the Hudson once were; who talks about the global elimination of smallpox between 1967 and 1977? If we did more, the world would undoubtedly be better; what we have done has sometimes kept it from becoming worse.

On the west side of the Sierra Nevada is the pristine land that would have become Mineral King, a huge Disney-owned ski complex, if the Sierra Club had not fought it. On the east is Mono Lake, which has had its tributaries restored and is halfway back to historic water levels after decades of being drained by Los Angeles. The Mono Lake Committee fought from 1979 to 1996 to get the court decision that restored the lake's water and still works to protect the lake. South of there, in the Mojave Desert, near the Old Woman Mountains, is Ward Valley, which was slated for a low-level nuclear waste dump that would've likely leaked all over creation. A beautiful coalition of the five local tribes, other local people, and antinuclear activists fought in the deserts and the courts and with the scientific facts for ten years before defeating it definitively a few years ago. On the West Texas–Mexican border is the small Latino community of Sierra Blanca, where another nuclear waste dump was planned but defeated. Go east to Oklahoma and you'll arrive in the sites where in 1993, after years of work, environmentalists, including the group Native Americans for a Clean Environment, and the Cherokee Nation shut down 23 percent of the world's uranium production. All these places are places of absence, or at least the absence of devastation, a few of the countless places in which there is nothing to see, and nothing is what victory often looks like.

The Angel of History says, "Terrible," but this angel says, "Could be worse." They're both right, but the latter angel gives us grounds to act.

14

Viagra for Caribou

The Old Testament God rules with a heavy hand over a static moral world, but I believe that our world is instead presided over by an alternate entity, Coyote, the Native American deity, an indestructible, lecherous, hilarious, and improvisational trickster, straying into and surviving catastrophe (a little like his simplified great-grandson, Chuck Jones's cartoon character Wile E. Coyote). Many North American creation myths do not portray a world that was perfect in the beginning. Instead, the world was made by flawed, humorous creators who never finished the job. In that world, there was never a state of grace, never a fall, and creation continues (which is why it's ironic, or maybe comic, that white people like to situate Native Americans in the frozen diorama of Eden before the Fall). In Yahweh's world, only the good do good, and only virtue is rewarded. Coyote's world is more complicated.

It turns out, for example, that Viagra is good for endangered species. Animal parts that traditional Chinese medicine prescribed as aphrodisiacs and for treating impotence—including from green turtles, seahorses, geckos, hooded and harp seals, and the velvet from the half-grown antlers of caribou—are, thanks to the drug, no longer in such demand. What more comic form of the mysterious unfolding of the world is there than this, which suggests that Viagra's ultimate purpose may be the survival of animals at the edges of the earth? Is the erotic toil of the Viagra-saturated not selfish but secretly on behalf of the caribou whose antlers are no longer being cut off while they're still tender, growing like small trees with blood for sap under that velvet? The sirocco winds carry the dust of African deserts to the humid parts of Europe, and another kind of wind, as powerful and amoral as a coyote fart, carries effects from Chinese bedrooms to Arctic tundra.

And in many places, the animals are coming back. There are wolves again in Yellowstone—and, as my friend Chip Ward asks, what kind of a species have we ourselves become to restore wolves to the places where we once strove so hard to eliminate them, to yearn to see or hear these creatures we once feared and hated? There are more buffalo on the Great Plains than at any time since the great annihilation of the 1870s, and the vision of creating "buffalo commons" hundreds or thousands of miles long may become a reality—in part because the region is losing its human population anyway. All over New England, as land that was farms in Thoreau's time and even in Robert Frost's goes feral and gets reforested, deer, moose, bears, cougars, coyotes, and other creatures are coming back in droves. Lyme disease, named after suburban Lyme, Connecticut, is a nationwide problem largely because deer populations skyrocketed and spread into suburbia everywhere from New England to the canyons of Los Angeles. It won't be the wilderness that it was—passenger pigeons will never blot out the sky again, just for starters—but it is more than anyone anticipated. Great blue herons nest in both New York's Central Park and San Francisco's Golden Gate Park, coyotes find their way into more and more cities, and ravens perch on the power lines outside my windows.

Wolves vanished from Britain in the mid-eighteenth century, bears several centuries before. There, last year, while people were discussing reintroducing the megafauna lost in previous centuries—the wolf, the bear, the lynx, the bison, the boar—the animals preempted them. A

herd of wild boar escaped the bounds of the Forest of Dean and established itself as truly wild—the fourth to do so, I read. I've talked to
an Irish wildlands administrator who hopes to reintroduce the wolves
that became extinct there two centuries earlier and read of the owners
of vast estates in Scotland eager to make their land the heart of this
carnivore-crowned wildness. As the nature writer Jim Crumley says,
"The last wolf in Scotland hasn't been born yet." Environmental historian Richard White tells of the return of hundreds of thousands of
sockeye salmon to Lake Washington in Seattle and of the enthusiasm
with which people greeted them. Their return was not, he adds, the re-
vitalization of an ancient salmon run; they were hatchery fish returning
to where scientists at the University of Washington had hatched them.
They were no pure ancient past coming back but they were one version
of a future with room in it for some kind of wildness. As White puts
it, "There is a hope in that for which we might gladly surrender purity."

The Angel of Alternate History asks us to believe in the invisible; Coyote asks us to trust in the basic eccentricity of the world, its
sense of humor, and its resilience. The moral worldview believes that
the good is accomplished through virtue, but sometimes army bases
become de facto wildlife preserves, sometimes virtue falls on its face.
Sometimes Las Vegas–style casinos give Native Americans visibility
and political clout. Sometimes corporations and the military demand
affirmative action because it benefits them too.

The Internet was invented by the US military and may be one of
our most valuable weapons against it, for the decentralized dissemi-
nation of information and for the organization of citizen action. The
Internet can be an elitist instrument, requiring access to computers—
and, usually, to electricity and phone lines—and the knowledge to use
them (though a nomadic friend tells me that all through the poorest
parts of the world—Thailand, Bolivia—the young flock to prolifer-
ating Internet cafes). But the Zapatistas were the first revolution to
make serious use of the Internet; the shutdown of the WTO meeting

in Seattle was organized to a significant extent by Internet communications, and so were the 2003 antiwar actions around the world. What can be said of a medium that sometimes seems to be made half out of cheesy porn sites and yet opens these doors? Just this: Coyote pisses on moral purity and rigid definitions.

15

Getting the Hell out
of Paradise

Perfection is a stick with which to beat the possible. Perfectionists can find fault with anything, and no one has higher standards in this regard than leftists. In January of 2003, when Republican governor George Ryan of Illinois overturned 167 death sentences, reprieving everyone on death row in that state, there were radical commentators who found fault with the details, carped when we should have been pouring champagne over our heads like football champs. But there's an increasing gap between this new movement, with its capacity for joy and carnival, and the old figureheads. Their grumpiness is often the grumpiness of perfectionists who hold that anything less than total victory is failure, a premise that makes it easy to give up at the start or to disparage the victories that are possible. This is Earth. It will never be heaven. There will always be cruelty, always be violence, always be destruction. There is tremendous devastation now. In the time it takes you to read this book, acres of rainforest will vanish, a species will go extinct, people will be raped, killed, dispossessed, die of easily preventable causes. We cannot eliminate all devastation for all time, but we can reduce it, outlaw it, undermine its sources and foundations: these are victories. A better world, yes; a perfect world, never.

A million years ago I wrote a few features for the punk magazine *Maximum Rocknroll*. One of them was about women's rights, and a cranky guy wrote in that women used to make sixty-six cents to the male dollar and now we made seventy-seven cents, so what were we complaining about? It doesn't seem like it should be so complicated to acknowledge that seventy-seven cents is better than sixty-six cents and that seventy-seven cents isn't good enough, but the politics we have is so pathetically bipolar that we only tell this story two ways: either seventy-seven cents is a victory, and victories are points where you shut up and stop fighting; or seventy-seven cents is ugly, so activism accomplishes nothing and what's the point of fighting? Both versions are defeatist because they are static. What's missing from these two ways of telling is an ability to recognize a situation in which you are traveling and have not arrived, in which you have cause both to celebrate and fight, in which the world is always being made and is never finished. What's missing, you could say, is a sense of Coyote's world instead of Yahweh's.

In South Africa, the apartheid system was overthrown after decades of heroic struggle of every kind, but economic justice has yet to arrive; it was a seventy-seven-cent victory. Vaclav Havel was a gorgeous gadfly to the Communists, but as president of Czechoslovakia and then the Czech Republic, he was just a seventy-seven-cent politician. "We are winning," said the graffiti in Seattle, not "We have won." It's a way of telling in which you can feel successful without feeling smug, in which you can feel challenged without feeling defeated. Most victories will be temporary, or incomplete, or compromised in some way, and we might as well celebrate them as well as the stunning victories that come from time to time. Without stopping. Even if someday we get to dollar-for-dollar parity, that will just free us up to attend to something else (just as US women's wages have advanced compared to men's, but most working people's wages and economic security have diminished overall since the 1970s). "Utopia is on the horizon," declares Eduardo Galeano. "When I walk two steps, it takes two steps back. I walk ten steps and it is ten steps further away. What is utopia for? It is for this, for walking."

Judeo-Christian culture's central story is of Paradise and the Fall. It is a story of perfection and of loss, and perhaps a deep sense of loss is contingent upon the belief in perfection. Conservatives rear-project narratives about how everyone used to be straight, god-fearing, decently clad and content with the nuclear family, narratives that any good reading of history undoes. Activists, even those who decry Judeo-Christian heritage as our own fall from grace, are as prone to tell the story of paradise, though their paradise might be matriarchal or vegan or the flip side of the technological utopia of classical socialism. And they compare the possible to perfection, again and again, finding fault with the former because of the latter. Paradise is imagined as a static place, as a place before or after history, after strife and eventfulness and change: the premise is that once perfection has arrived change is no longer necessary. This idea of perfection is also why people believe in saving, in going home, and in activism as crisis response rather than everyday practice.

Moths and other nocturnal insects navigate by the moon and stars. Those heavenly bodies are useful for them to find their way, even though they never get far from the surface of the earth. But lightbulbs and candles send them astray; they fly into the heat or the flame and die. For these creatures, to arrive is a calamity. When activists mistake heaven for some goal at which they must arrive, rather than an idea to navigate Earth by, they burn themselves out, or they set up a totalitarian utopia in which others are burned in the flames. Don't mistake a lightbulb for the moon, and don't believe that the moon is useless unless we land on it. After all those millennia of poetry about the moon, nothing was more prosaic than the guys in space suits stomping around on the moon with their flags and golf clubs thirty-something years ago. The moon is profound *except* when we land on it.

Paradise is not the place in which you arrive but the journey toward it. Sometimes I think victories must be temporary or incomplete; what kind of humanity would survive paradise? The industrialized world has tried to approximate paradise in its suburbs, with luxe, calme, volupté, cul-de-sacs, cable television and two-car garages, and it has produced a soft ennui that shades over into despair and a decay of the soul suggesting that Paradise is already a gulag. Countless desperate teenagers will tell you so. For paradise does not require of us courage, selflessness, creativity, passion: paradise in all accounts is passive, is sedative, and if you read carefully, soulless.

That's why John Keats called the world with all its suffering "this vale of soul-making," why crisis often brings out the best in us. Some imaginative Christian heretics worshipped Eve for having liberated us from paradise—the myth of the fortunate fall. The heretics recognized that before the fall we were not yet fully human—in Paradise, Adam and Eve need not wrestle with morality, with creation, with society, with mortality; they only realize their own humanity in the struggle an imperfect world invites. When the Iraq War broke out, we in San Francisco shut down downtown, shut down streets, bridges, highways, corporations that first day and kept coming back for weeks. Out of all that conviction, all that passion, one thing stood out for me: Gopal Dayaneni, one of the key organizers for the antiwar actions, was asked by the daily newspaper why he was getting arrested. "I have a soul," he replied.

Recent strains of activism proceed on the realization that victory is not some absolute state far away but the achieving of it, not the moon landing but the flight. A number of ideas and practices have emerged that live this out. The term "politics of prefiguration" has long been used to describe the idea that if you embody what you aspire to, you have already succeeded. That is to say, if your activism is already democratic, peaceful, creative, then in one small corner of the world these things have triumphed. Activism, in this model, is not only a toolbox to change things but a home in which to take up residence and live according to your beliefs, even if it's a temporary and local place, this paradise of participating, this vale where souls get made.

This has been an important belief for activists who recognize that change happens as much by inspiration and catalyst as by imposition. You could describe activism as having two primary strains: the attempt to change something problematic outside itself and the attempt to build something better, though the two strains are irrevocably and necessarily intertangled, which is exactly the point of the politics of prefiguration. The idea was itself prefigured by Walter Benjamin, who wrote, "The class struggle . . . is a fight for the crude and material things without which no refined and spiritual things could exist. Nevertheless, it is not in the forms of the spoils which fall to the victor that the latter make their presence felt in the class struggle. They manifest themselves in this struggle as courage, humor, cunning, and fortitude." They are present all along the journey; arrival is at best irrelevant, at worst undermining, at least to the goods of the spirit. Reclaim the Streets (RTS), the rowdy British movement of the later 1990s, lived this out beautifully. The premise behind RTS's street parties seemed to be that if what they were protesting against was isolation, privatization, and alienation, then a free-for-all party out in public was not just a protest but a solution, if a solution in the mode that Hakim Bey called "Temporary Autonomous Zones." (Bey contrasted these moments of liberation with revolutions proper, which "lead to the expected curve, the consensus-approved trajectory: revolution, reaction, betrayal, the founding of a stronger and even more oppressive State . . . By failing to follow this curve, the *up-rising* suggests the possibility of a movement outside and beyond the Hegelian spiral of that 'progress' which is secretly nothing more than a vicious circle.") RTS and the antiroads movement took on what could be called the postindustrialization of

Britain, the privatization of everyday life and the imposition of monster roads and freeways on still-vital landscapes and communities.

There were some beautiful moments: people taking up residence in trees, in which they established legal residence by receiving mail there, a tactic to keep the tree from being cut; an RTS party in which they surged onto a freeway overpass and, muffled by rave music, smuggled jackhammers onto the concrete under the giant bell-skirt of a stilt-walking grande dame, then jackhammered openings in which trees were planted; huge street parties in downtown London that linked up with activists around the world to become global anticapitalist demonstrations. Humor, creativity, outrageousness, and exuberance were among the group's hallmarks. That RTS didn't outlive its moment was also a kind of victory, a recognition that time had moved on and the focus was elsewhere. Instead, RTS's incendiary carnival spirit, global Internet communications, and tactics of temporary victory became part of the vocabulary of what came next, the global justice movement. RTS decomposed itself into the soil from which new flowers sprung.

One day in California, I hear a Zen Buddhist abbot from Ireland quote the Argentinian Jorge Luis Borges, "There is no day without its moments of paradise." And then the day continues.

16

Across the Great Divide

The poet and polemicist June Jordan once wrote,

> We should take care so that we will lose none of the jewels of our soul. We must begin, now, to reject the white, either/or system of dividing the world into unnecessary conflict. For example, it is tragic and ridiculous to choose between Malcolm X and Dr. King: each of them hurled himself against a quite different aspect of our predicament, and both of them, literally, gave their lives to our ongoing struggle. We need everybody and all that we are.

Jordan asks us to give up the dividing by which we conquer ourselves, the sectarianism, the presumption that difference is necessarily opposition. So does the activism of the moment.

That arrival of the millennium I tried to delineate could be told another way, as the departure of the binaries and oppositions by which we used to imagine the world. The end of the Soviet Bloc meant that capitalism and communism no longer defined a world of difference or a political standoff that had long been described as east versus west. The Zapatistas came along five years later with a politic that was neither capitalist nor communist, but implicitly positioned them together as means of displacing power from the individual, the community, the local. Opposition is often illusory: the old distinction between

Aristotelians and Platonists, for example, overlooks how similar these two camps might be to a Taoist or a shaman. Gender, once imagined as a pair of definitive opposites, has been reimagined as a spectrum of anatomies, affinities, and attractions.

Another binary that has become outdated is right and left. Though these terms are still deployed all the time, what do they define? They derive from how the French National Assembly seated itself a few years after the revolution of 1789: the more radical sat on the left, and thus radicals have been leftists ever since. Seating arrangements, however, have changed since the eighteenth century. They've changed a lot in the last fifteen years. Or perhaps we've all stood up at last and begun to move somewhere new, somewhere unknown. The term "leftist" carries with it a baggage of socialism, utopianism, and sometimes authoritarianism that no longer delimits (and never quite did) what radicals and revolutionaries might be. Anarchists and communists can be far more different than Platonists and Aristotelians. And there are a lot of people who might embrace every item in a leftist platform except identification with the left and its legacy.

As the Republicans move from what might be conventionally thought of as right-wing to something a little more totalitarian, as the New Labour administration finds a low point in the middle for what used to be the party of the left, there are dissenters on both sides. There have been strange moments before: animal-rights activists pursuing anti-environmental goals; feminists supporting restrictions on the free speech of abortion protesters and pornographers; all these suggest that there are far more than two political positions, and the old terminology only blinds us.

I've often wondered what alliances and affinities might arise without those badges of right and left. For example, the recent American militia movements were patriarchal, nostalgic, nationalist, gun-happy, and full of weird fantasies about the UN, but they had something in common with us: they prized the local and feared its erasure by the transnational. The guys drilling with guns might've been too weird to be our allies, but they were just the frothy foam on a big wave of alienation, suspicion and fear from people watching their livelihoods and their communities go down the tubes. What could have happened if we could have spoken directly to the people in that wave, if we could have found common ground, if we could have made our position neither right nor left but truly grassroots? What would have happened if we had given them an alternate version of how local power was being sapped, by whom, and what they might do about it? We need them, we need a broad base, we need a style that speaks to far more people than the left has lately been able to speak to and for.

And without going too far into the ninety-car pileup the late sixties resembles to one who was playing with plastic horsies during that era, it does seem that the countercultural left hijacked progressive politics and made it into something that was almost guaranteed to alienate most working people. I grew up in that left encouraged to despise "rednecks and white trash"—the racism of some working-class white Southerners became a handy way for the middle class elsewhere to carry on class war while feeling progressive. Activists are still trying to shed the stereotypes the media made out of the white-radical sixties, the image in which all us activists are spoiled, sneering, unpatriotic, and sometimes violent hotheads. Of course, all activism nowadays is indebted to the other versions of what the sixties was, from the highly visible civil rights movement to the many grassroots activists who are still active.

This is part of what made Seattle so significant in 1999: the unions represented at least some rapprochement of blue-collar industrial America with environmentalists, anarchists, indigenous activists and farmers from Korea to France. Farmers around the world are being ravaged by free trade, which has radicalized many of them and created new alliances, new activism, movements such as the hundred-nation coalition Via Campesino, with its hundred million members. The activist-theorist John Jordan points out that just as a wonderful coalition was born when Mexican leftists went into Chiapas and found common ground with the indigenous population, so farmer Jose Bové and his peers were revolutionaries who formed similar liaisons in the French countryside. In the American West, something similar has been happening, something that partakes of the same open-mindedness, of the best part of politics' strange bedfellows, happy in bed together, working out their differences. What gets called the left has often had as its principal hallmark being right, a sectarian righteousness that is also dissipating to make room for some spectacular new tactics, movements, and coalitions.

At Citizen Alert's 1996 board retreat in remote Eureka, Nevada, we all ended up drinking at the anti-environmentalist bar because it was the only one in town with beer on tap. The purple WRANGLER t-shirts for sale behind the bar spelled out the acronym—Western Ranchers Against No Good Leftist Environmentalist Radical Shitheads. That evening I ended up on a stool next to a young rancher in a large hat who thought environmentalists hated him. As it turned out, his family has been ranching in the area for generations, he was knowledgeable about sustainable and rotational grazing if not about the nifty new terminology for it and boasted that his grass grazed the bellies of his cows, unlike all the hit-and-run ranchers nearby *he* deplored and the mining corporations he deplored more. By the end of the evening I'd convinced him that some environmentalists thought he might be just fine, and he was buying me whiskey.

He wasn't paranoid. The wise-use and private property–rights movements, like the militias, have done a much better job of reaching out to rural communities than progressives and environmentalists have. For a long time a lot of environmentalists demonized ranchers. It was a truism that cattle were ravaging the American West, until environmentalists in various places realized that sometimes ranchers were holding the line on open space: when ranchers were forced out, development came in. Some cattle ranching was devastating the landscape; some was being better managed; and new ideas about riparian protection, rotational grazing, fire ecology, and other rangeland management practices have been improving the ways grazing land can be cared for.

Ranch families generally love their land and know it with an intimacy few environmentalists will arrive at; some have been there for a century and want to be there for another one. And they too, like farmers everywhere, are being afflicted by price drops produced by globalization and the industrialization of the rural (the factory-like corporate systems for producing meat, vegetables, and grains). They are a mostly unrecruited constituency of the global justice movement, in contrast to many other countries where farmers are already the backbone. In the past decade a number of alliances have formed in the United States, from groups like the Nature Conservancy working with ranchers to create land trusts and conservation easements to environmentalist–rancher coalitions. Widespread coalbed methane drilling in Wyoming has devastated a lot of ranches and pushed Republican ranchers into coalition with environmentalists, as have sprawl, resort development, water crises, and the need to restore depleted land in Colorado, New Mexico, and Arizona.

Environmentalists had worked with a purist paradigm of untouched versus ravaged nature. Working with ranchers opened up the possibility of a middle way, one in which categories were porous, humans have a place in the landscape—in working landscapes, not just white-collar vacation landscapes—and activism isn't necessarily oppositional. This represents a big shift in the class politics of the once awfully white-collar environmental movement, which has been pretty good at alienating people who actually live in the environment and work with the resources in question. For the West, this means the undoing of a huge dichotomy, a huge cultural war, and a reinvention of how change works. For all of us it represents a new kind of activism in which coalitions can be based on what wildly different groups have in common and differences can be set aside; a coalition requires difference as a cult does not, and sometimes it seems like the ideological litmus tests of earlier movements moved them toward cultism.

Arizona environmentalist-rancher Bill McDonald, cofounder of the Malpai Borderlands Group, may have been the one to coin the term "the radical center," the space in which ranchers, environmentalists, and government agencies have been able to work together and to see the preservation of rural livelihoods and the land itself as the same goal. The Quivera Coalition in New Mexico is the most visible example, but many small organizations around the West have been working in this center. Lynne Sherrod, who ranches near Steamboat Springs, Colorado, and heads the Colorado Cattlemen's Agricultural Land Trust, recalls, "The environmentalists and the ranchers were squared off against one another, and while we were fighting, the developers were walking off with the valley . . . We found out we had a lot more in common than what kept us apart."

Classical environmentalism is interventionist and oppositional: it uses pressure, law, and lawsuits to prevent others from acting. The radical center, as writer and New Mexico land manager William DeBuys defines it, is "a departure from business as usual," is, he continues,

> not bigoted. By that I mean that, to do this kind of work, you don't question where somebody is from or what kind of hat he or she wears, you focus on where that person is willing to go and whether he or she is willing to work constructively on matters of mutual interest. Work in the Radical Center also involves a commitment to using a diversity of tools. There is no one way of doing things. We need to have large toolboxes and to lend and borrow tools freely. Work in the Radical Center is experimental—it keeps developing new alternatives every step along the way. Nothing is ever so good that it can't stand a little revision, and nothing is ever so impossible and broken down that a try at fixing it is out of the question.

It's a hopeful practice, since where litigious activism saw enemies it sees potential allies. It's a peacemaking practice, in contrast to the warlike modes of intervention. It isn't the right answer to everything—nothing is—but it's a significant new model.

As are the legendary Ohio farmworker-organizer Baldemar Velasquez's subversive tactics. Velasquez, the founder of the Farm Labor Organizing Committee, says, "Number one, I don't consider anybody opposition. I just consider anyone either misinformed or miseducated or downright wrong-thinking. That's the way I look at people, and I believe that what we do, getting justice for migrant workers is the good and right thing in life to do and everyone ought to be on our side." Velasquez talks directly to those who might be considered the opposition and sometimes brings them over, a tactic that has stood him in good stead in a number of organizing battles, as have his boycotts of Campbell's Soup and other food corporations. "It's not what you serve up but how you serve it up," he told me. "The way you win people over to your side is try to present the information from some perspective they're familiar with."

In one case, he got a lot of children of Christian Republicans in a Toledo, Ohio, religious school to join him by preaching to them from the Bible. An ordained minister, Velasquez describes the experience:

> [I] opened up the book right in front of this big assembly of high-school and junior-high kids, five hundred or so kids in the auditorium, and said, "Let's see what God's word has to say . . . It says that there are three groups of people God watches over jealously in the entire history of scripture, the orphans, the widows, the aliens. And how many of you want to do something about these three groups of people God watches over very jealously?" Every kid in the auditorium raised their hands. Then I asked them to do three things.

He got them to fast during lunchtime and donate their lunch money to the widow and children of a Mexican farmworker who'd died horribly

in this country. He got them to educate their parents and congrega-
tions, got eight of the kids to join him in taking the money they raised
to the family in a Nahuatl Indian village in the Mexican mountains,
where they saw firsthand the poverty that sends immigrants to the
United States. And then he got more than three hundred of these
children of conservative Christians to join him in a protest of the supermarkets selling the pickles that were the subject of a farmworkers'
battle. He won that battle too, prompting many supermarkets to stop
carrying the brand, thereby forcing the pickle growers to keep the crop
in Ohio and to treat farmworkers as employees rather than sharecrop-
pers. He's worked with international labor issues, with environmental
justice issues, with the larger networks within which farmworkers toil.
But what makes him remarkable is this making of connections not just
between issues but between sides.

17

After Ideology,
or Alterations in Time

I n important ways, these little ripples of inspired activism around
the United States parallel aspects of the global justice movement
and the Zapatistas. All three share an improvisational, collaborative,
creative process that is in profound ways anti-ideological, if ideology means ironclad preconceptions about who's an ally and how to
make a better future. There's an openheartedness, a hopefulness and
a willingness to change and to trust. Cornel West came up with the
idea of the jazz freedom fighter and defined jazz "not so much as a
term for a musical art form but for a mode of being in the world, an
improvisational mode of protean, fluid and flexible disposition toward
reality suspicious of 'either/or' viewpoints." That similar journeys beyond binary logic and rigid ideology should be happening in such
different arenas suggests that when we talk about a movement we
are not talking about a specific population or a specific agenda but a
zeitgeist, a change in the air.

Or perhaps we should not talk about a movement, or movements,
but about movement: to apprehend these wild changes is as though to
see many, many groups of people get up and move around from the

positions they sat in so long. Charles Derber calls this the "third wave," claiming it as a successor to the first wave of 1960s-style activism and the second wave of fragmented identity politics: "While the third wave has begun serious new political thinking about global alternatives, it is basically antidoctrinal, in contrast to both the first and second waves. This reflects the huge variety of global constituencies and the need to accommodate their many issues and points of view. Resisting a 'party line' has kept the movement together." To be antidoctrinal is to open yourself up to new and unexpected alliances, to new networks of power. It's to reject the static utopia in favor of the improvisational journey. Just as the environmental movement is the beneficiary of an enormously more sophisticated understanding of natural systems, so activism benefits from the mistakes, inspirations, and tools provided by past movements.

Naomi Klein remarked about global justice activists a few years ago,

> When critics say the protesters lack vision, what they are really saying is that they lack an overarching revolutionary philosophy—like Marxism, democratic socialism, deep ecology or social anarchy—on which they all agree. That is absolutely true, and for this we should be extraordinarily thankful. At the moment, the anti-corporate street activists are ringed by would-be leaders, anxious to enlist them as foot soldiers for their particular cause. It is to this young movement's credit that it has as yet fended off all of these agendas and has rejected everyone's generously donated manifesto.

Elsewhere she described Marcos and the Zapatistas in terms that exactly fit the loose networks of anarchist global justice activists: "non-hierarchical decision-making, decentralized organizing, and deep community democracy." This is an ideology of sorts, but an ideology of absolute democracy that's about preventing authority from rising, with the concomitant limits on imagination, participation, adaptation, which is to say that it is an ideology against ideologies. If there were purist or puritan tendencies in earlier waves of activism, this is generously, joyously impure, with the impurity that comes from mixing and circulating and stirring things up.

From deep inside that realm my London-based friend John Jordan, a wonderful writer and activist—part of Reclaim the Streets then, of the global justice movement now—writes me,

> Our movements are trying to create a politics that challenges all the certainties of traditional leftist politics, not by replacing them with new ones, but by dissolving any notion that we have answers, plans or strategies that are watertight or universal. In fact our strategies must be more like water itself, undermining everything that is fixed, hard and rigid with fluidity, constant movement and evolution. We are trying to build a politics of process, where the only certainty is doing what feels right at the right time and in the right place—a politics that doesn't wait (interesting how wait and hope are the same words in Spanish) but acts in the moment, not to create something in the future but to build in the present, it's the politics of the here and now. When we are asked how are we going to build a new world, our answer is, "We don't know, but let's build it together." In effect we are saying the end is not as important as the means, we are turning hundreds of years of political form and content on its head by putting the means before the ends, by putting context in front of ideology, by rejecting purity and perfection, in fact, we are turning our backs on the future.
>
> It's an enormous challenge, because in a chaotic world people need something to hold onto and something to hold them, if all is uncertain, if uncertainty is the only certainty, then the uprooted, the fragile, those that crave something to give them meaning in their lives, simply get washed away by the flood and flux of an unsure universe. For them, hope is often found in certainty. Not necessarily certainty rooted in a predictable future, but certainty that they are doing the right thing with their lives . . . Taking power has been the goal at the end of the very straight and narrow road of most

political movements of the past. Taking control of the future lies at the root of nearly every historical social change strategy, and yet we are building movements which believe that to "let go" is the most powerful thing we can do—to let go, walk away from power and find freedom. Giving people back their creative agency, reactivating their potential for a direct intervention into the world is at the heart of the process. With agency and meaning reclaimed, perhaps it is possible to imagine tomorrow today and to be wary of desires that can only be fulfilled by the future. In that moment of creation, the need for certainty is subsumed by the joy of doing, and the doing is filled with meaning.

Jordan's vision is widely shared. The philosopher Alphonso Lingus says, "We really have to free the notion of liberation and revolution from the idea of permanently setting up some other kind of society." Subcommandante Marcos understands well that what older revolutionary movements would have considered victory would be defeat for the Zapatistas, and he calls Zapatismo "not an ideology but an intuition." Zapatista scholar John Holloway has a manifesto of a book out called *Change the World Without Taking Power*, a similar argument that the revolution is an end in itself that fails its spirit and its ideals when it becomes the next institutional power. As my brother David, a global justice organizer, sums up Holloway's position,

> The notion of capturing positions of power, either through elections or insurrection, misses the point that the aim of revolution is to fundamentally change the relations of power. There is a vast area of do-it-yourself activity directed towards changing the world that does not have the state as its focus and that does not aim at gaining positions of power. It is an arena in which the old distinctions between reform and revolution no longer seem relevant, simply because the question of who controls the state is not the focus of attention.

This is what the Temporary Autonomous Zones, the politics of pre-figuration, the adage about "process not product" have all been inching toward, a revolution in the nature of revolution, with the promise that whatever mistakes we make, they will not be the same old ones.

Sandinista poet Giaconda Belli writes that July 18 and 19, 1979, when the Sandinista rebels overthrew the Somoza dictatorship in Nicaragua, were "two days that felt as if a magical, age-old spell had been cast over us, taking us back to Genesis, to the very site of the creation of the world." These other versions of what revolution means suggest that the goal is not so much to go on and create the world as to live in that time of creation, and with this the emphasis shifts from institutional power to the power of consciousness and the enactments of daily life, toward a revolution that does not institute its idea of perfection but opens up the freedom for each to participate in inventing the world. Revolutionary moments, as Belli evinces, have an extraordinary intensity, the intensity of living in history, of feeling the power to make one's life and make the world, the communion between people liberated from the bonds that limit and separate them. "Revolutionary moments are carnivals in which the individual life celebrates its unification with a regenerated society," wrote Situationist Raoul Vaneigem. The question, then, is not so much how to create the world as how to keep alive that moment of creation, how to realize that Coyote world in which creation never ends and people participate in the power of being creators, a world whose hopefulness lies in its unfinishedness, its openness to improvisation and participation. The revolutionary days I have been outlining are days in which hope is no longer fixed on the future: it becomes an electrifying force in the present.

18

The Global Local,
or Alterations in Place

A decade or so ago I was repeating to my aunt the then-current critique of the 1955 blockbuster exhibition and book *The Family of Man*. It was popular to denigrate it for its insistence on a universal humanity painted in the broadest terms, its photographs suggesting that motherhood or voting or work was ultimately the same everywhere, in disregard of the differences that postmodernism and multiculturalism have emphasized. My aunt exclaimed, "You don't understand what it was like then, how divided we were, how important it was to find common ground after the war and the Holocaust and with the racism that was still rampant." The focus on the local of late has been a counterbalance not only to the universalizing "truths" of modernism but to the homogenizing, power-consolidating forces of corporate culture and agriculture.

But the political commentator Danny Postel writes, "As the Egyptian sociologist and dissident Saad Eddin Ibrahim has noted, when human rights activists from different countries get together and exchange notes, they invariably find that, despite wide geographic, cultural and religious chasms, they share many of the same experiences and speak a remarkably common idiom." The answer to most either/or questions is both; the best response to a paradox is to embrace both sides instead of cutting off one or the other for the sake of coherence. The question is about negotiating a viable relationship between the local and the global, not signing up with one and shutting out the other.

One way to define the global justice movement of our time is as a global movement in defense of the local—of local food, local jurisdiction over labor and resources, local production, local culture, local species, domesticated and wild, of the protection of environments that are by definition local. The old slogan that went "Think globally, act locally" could be stood on its head as "Think locally, act globally," for the local is one way to describe what's under assault by transnational corporations, but the resistance is often globally networked. Much of the radicalism of our time is in celebration and defense of the local—but it would be too simple to set up the local as the good. Think of how the civil rights movement appealed to the federal government to dismantle the South's local customs of apartheid, intimidation, and voter exclusion or, nowadays, of the many Westerners who resent the federal government for interfering with their perceived right to assault the local environment for fun and profit. Sometimes broader forces counteract a malignant local.

In the period my aunt spoke of, a racialist-nationalist localism had devastated the world. In our time, a lot of the devastation is wrought by and for transnational capital, to which the local serves as a counterbalance. The local can mean human scale, a scale on which people can be heard, make a difference, understand the dynamics of power and hold it accountable—a democratizing impulse. In the 1970s, mostly in rural places, mostly on the West Coast, some attempted to return to and to rethink the local (which other cultures had never left), in the movement or tendency called bioregionalism. It was an attempt to live within the potential meanings, communities, limitations, and long-term prospects of a region, to live on local terms, eat local foods, to know exactly where you were and how to take care of it. It was about belonging to a place not as a birthright but as an act of conscious engagement. In some ways bioregionalism prefigures the anti-ideologicalism of the present in that it was about adapting rather than imposing, and its emphasis on the local meant that it wasn't preaching a gospel that could be exported without alteration. Imposition is about consolidation of power; the local I'm interested in is about dispersing it.

A dozen years ago, the environmental writer and trickster Jim Dodge remarked, "I'm not so sure bioregionalism even has a doctrine to be pure about—it's more a sense of direction (uphill, it seems) than the usual leftist highway to Utopia . . ." Bioregionalism was an attempt to return to what human life had been for most of history, ecologically and socially, to return not nostalgically but radically, with a sense that this could also be the future, that it was the only viable future. Though you don't hear much about bioregionalism anymore, its ideals are present in the slow food movement, the farmers' markets springing up everywhere in the United States and Britain, the emphases on eating locally and seasonally, environmentally sound building practices, sustainable urban designs and systems for garbage, water, and power, and in the revivals that celebrate and maintain local culture and memory amid the homogenization that is corporate globalization's cultural impact.

Dodge claims anarchy as an essential element of bioregionalism, "the conviction that we as a community, or a tight, small-scale federation of communities, can mind our own business, and can make decisions regarding our individual and communal lives and gladly accept the responsibilities and consequences of those decisions." This brings us back to the activism of the past twenty years. Or more, since contemporary anarchist organizing draws upon the decentralized models of the anarchists of the Spanish Civil War for its affinity groups, the more or less autonomous associations of five to fifteen people that constitute the basic unit of direct action. "The center cannot hold," wrote Yeats, and "mere anarchy is loosed upon the world," but that is finally starting to look like a good thing for anarchists and localists who didn't trust the centralization of power (particularly since that "blood-dimmed tide" is loosed by centralized authorities as much as anyone).

In other words, they were, or rather we are, anarchists, and this mode of organizing comes most directly out of the antinuclear movement of the 1980s, where direct democracy was established through affinity groups and spokescouncils using consensus decision-making processes (a spokescouncil is a meeting to which member affinity groups have each sent a spokesperson). *Anarchy* is an incendiary word that might be better set aside, and it comes from a Eurocentric history that doesn't encompass, for example, traditional participatory cultures, which are equally important as sources and presences, and in which membership in the community counterbalances and channels the rights of individuals. Another way to describe a lot of this nameless movement is as a resurgence of antihierarchical direct democracy—the dispersal or localization of power. In Argentina, which since December 2001 has had a severe economic crisis and an inspired rise of neighborhood and community groups to replace failed institutions, it's called *horizontalidad*, or horizontality. Perhaps it's all just democracy at its most potent.

The embrace of local power doesn't have to mean parochialism, withdrawal, or intolerance, only a coherent foundation from which to navigate the larger world. From the wild coalitions of the global justice movement to the cowboys and environmentalists sitting down together, there is an ease with difference that doesn't need to be eliminated, a sense that if the essentials of principle or goal are powerful enough you can work together, and that perhaps differences are a strength, not a weakness. A sense that you can have an identity embedded in local circumstance and a role in the global dialogue, an interest in networks of connection and a loss of faith in the reality of clear-cut borders. And this global dialogue exists in service of the local. The Maori of New Zealand have had significant success in reviving their language, and Native Hawaiians have modeled their language programs after the Maori and in turn become models for the wave of language preservations and promulgations across Native North America. So this other globalization, the globalization of communication and of ideas, can be the antithesis of the homogenization and consolidation brought by the spread of chains and brands and corporations. It can be the small in opposition to the big: Arundhati Roy writes of "the dismantling of the Big—big bombs, big dams, big ideologies, big contradictions, big heroes, big mistakes. Perhaps it will be the Century of the Small."

The best way to resist a monolithic institution or corporation is not with a monolithic movement but with multiplicity itself. Of course the big story is Fox News in the United States, Rupert Murdoch's empire in the English-speaking world, Prime Minister Berlusconi's media monopoly in Italy, the great consolidations, but the little stories are a hundred thousand websites, listservs, and blogs on the net, the hundreds of Indymedia sites around the world launched in kinship with the Seattle 1999 mothersite, and so forth. The counter to Monsanto Corporation's genetic engineering and agricultural patents isn't just anti-GMO and antipatenting activism and legislation, it's local farmers, farmers' markets, seed diversity, organic crops, integrated pest management, and other practices that work best on the small scale. A farmers' market selling the produce of local farmers isn't an adequate solution but ten thousand of them begin to be. This creates alternatives that are far less visible and individually far less powerful; domination by Monsanto is news in a way that the arrival of the first chiles or peaches at the farmers' market is not. The purpose of activism and art, or at least of mine, is to make a world in which people are producers of meaning, not consumers, and writing this book I now see how this is connected to the politics of hope and to those revolutionary days that are the days of creation of the world. Decentralization and direct democracy could, in one definition, be this politic in which people are producers, possessed of power and vision, in an unfinished world.

19

A Dream Three Times
the Size of Texas

I have long been fascinated by October 12, 1992, the five hundredth anniversary of Christopher Columbus's arrival in the Americas. The initial plans for the Columbian quincentennial were overwhelmed by opposition to that celebration of colonialism. Indigenous people throughout the Western Hemisphere used the occasion—not just a single day but a discussion that began long before and continues yet—to assert their own history of the Americas, as a place that was not discovered but invaded. Invaded but not quite conquered, for though much was lost, the quincentennial was an occasion for many native groups to assert that they are still here, that they remember, and that this history is not over.

Thus the quincentennial became an occasion for many non-natives to relearn the genocidal history of the Americas and sometimes address those parts of the history still with us—questions of sovereignty, visibility, representation, reparation, and land rights, among other things. Thus, remembering the past became the grounds to make change in the present. Thus, culture becomes politics. In the end, the day did not commemorate the start of an era but marked in some subtle way the beginning of its end. Perhaps I should have counted October 12, 1992, as one of the key moments of the millennium—except that what mattered most didn't happen just on that day but all around it.

After the Second World War, one of the programs to dissolve Native Americans' identity, diffuse their power, and detach them from their land base involved resettling them in the cities to assimilate. For many, cities instead gave them access to new resources and information and fostered intertribal political alliances. Out of this, in Minneapolis, came the American Indian movement (AIM) in 1968 (and, of course, out of the hope for justice and tactics for achieving it offered by the civil rights movement and out of the carnival of the later 1960s). Out of an AIM conference in 1974 came the International Indian Treaty Council. In 1977, the treaty council went to the United Nations, where it became the first indigenous organization to apply for and receive non-governmental—NGO—status. So you can trace the quincentennial back to 1974, or 1968, or for that matter 1492, along a zigzag trail of encounters, reactions, and realizations.

Treaty council activist Roxanne Dunbar-Ortiz was at the UN General Assembly in 1980, when Spain proposed that 1992 be declared the "year of encounter of civilizations" and "it was the most amazing thing—every African government representative stood up and walked out, so I walked out. They were not thinking about indigenous people, but this was the onset of slavery and they sure knew that." South Africa's African National Congress and African NGOs would prove important allies for the UN-based struggle for indigenous rights. Spain had planted the idea of the quincentennial of Columbus's arrival, but indigenous-rights activists would reshape it into an antithesis of Spain's agenda.

"We never got one single line of media attention," says Dunbar-Ortiz of the early years. Getting the word out was "just really hard work" carried out by speakers traveling to reservations, groups, and conferences, and by publishing a newsletter put together by the poet Simon Ortiz, among others. Word spread, and ideas began to shift. Dunbar-Ortiz told me, "It is exactly what gives you hope when you see this happen— when you see how hungry people are for the truth. When it is offered to them, they seize it." Ideas have been at least as important as law in the shift of status of indigenous Americans, for even the legal gains seem to be built on a foundation of changed imagination and rewritten history. Columbus Day became an occasion to rethink the past, and rethinking the past opened the way to a different future.

Nonindigenous Americans often embraced two contradictory not-so-true stories before that change. One was that Native Americans had all been wiped out—the tale of how a frail, static people had been swept away by progress was sometimes told sadly, but seldom questioned. Even radicals seemed in love with this tragedy, and again and again books casually assert some tribe or nation has vanished that hasn't. We had the end of the trail, the last of the Mohicans, a vanishing race, a dying nation, a doomed people, stories that might condemn the past but let us off the hook for unfinished conflicts. In the other key story, there never had been any Native Americans, because the continent had been pristine, untouched, virgin wilderness before we got here, a story particularly dear to environmentalists who saw nature as a nonhuman realm, a place apart. Putting Native Americans back in the picture meant radically redefining what nature means and what the human place in it might be (another undoing of a dichotomy, the nature–culture divide, with profound implications for the environmental movement, which has not yet altogether come to terms with this revision of meaning). Putting them in the present meant that the Indian wars were not over. The difference is that in recent years they have begun to win, some things, some of the time, and that this time the wars are mostly in the courts, the Congress, over textbooks, novels, movies, monuments, museums, and mascots, as well as on and over the land.

The quincentennial became an opportunity to restate what Columbus's arrival had meant—invasion, colonialism, genocide—and what it had been met with—"Five hundred years of resistance" was the catch-phrase. Other factors, from academic discourse to the legal ruling that allowed Native American casinos pop up across the United States (you can't lose your shirt to an extinct people), shifted the terms of native visibility and historical memory. But it was the quincentennial that had made the Zapatistas say "*basta*," enough, and decide to emerge from hiding fifteen months later. And it was probably the quincentennial conversation, as well as the brutal civil war in Guatemala, that moved the Nobel Committee to give the Nobel Peace Prize to indigenous Guatemalan human-rights activist Rigoberta Menchú.

Since then, a surge of indigenous power has transformed the face of politics in many Latin American states, including Columbia, Ecuador, Peru, and Bolivia. For example, in 2000, Ecuadoran General Lucio Gutierrez was ordered to repress protests against government policy by tens of thousands of indigenous Ecuadorians. Instead, he set up kitchens to feed them, permitted them to occupy the Congress, and joined an indigenous leader in announcing a new government. He was jailed for this disobedience, kicked out of the army—and in 2002 he was elected president, the first time indigenous people had exercised such power anywhere in the hemisphere. Far from perfect, he still represents a crucial shift in power.

Gutierrez was elected a month after the 510th anniversary of Columbus's arrival, which became another day of hemispheric action stretching from Canada to Chile, ten months before the victory in Cancun led in part by indigenous Yucatan farmers. In the United States, the gains have been on many fronts, from the repatriation of indigenous corpses and skeletons in museum collections to lawsuits against the Department of the Interior for "losing" billions of dollars that belong to the tribes, along with the records of that money. The number of people in the United States identifying as Native American more than doubled between the 1990 and 2000 censuses, in part because the new census recognized mixed-race identities, but also because far more people were willing to acknowledge an identity that had once been denigrated. From being a dying race, the indigenous peoples of the Americas have become a growing force.

The Coast Miwok were supposed to be extinct when I was growing up on their territory; in 1992 they began fighting for federal recognition, and in 2000, led by the gifted part-Miwok novelist Greg Sarris, they got it. In Yosemite National Park, the cradle of the concept of virgin nature, the Native people who were wiped out of the official representations—park signage, park histories, land management policies—have in the past decade reappeared in those contested cultural sites. And they've won the right to build their own cultural center in the park, a small victory for them but a big shift in defining what nature might mean and who will define it for the four million visitors per year. The Timbisha Shoshone, whose homeland became Death Valley National Park, have won far more. In 1994 they won federal recognition of their status as a tribe with unextinguished rights, and in 2000 they gained jurisdiction over nearly eight thousand acres in the park, as well as extensive lands outside the park. Some of the Nez Perce recently returned to their eastern Oregon homeland after 120 years in exile and made peace with the whites living there.

And this scale is dwarfed by other victories. The Inuit activist John Amagoalik remembers that in the 1960s journalists would come to his Arctic homeland and write about it as "a wasteland where nobody lives . . . There was always agreement between them that Inuit could not survive as a people. They all agreed that Inuit culture and language 'will disappear.'" On April 1, 1999, the Inuit got their homeland back. They won from the Canadian government their own autonomously governed province, Nunavut, a huge tract of far northeastern land three times the size of Texas, ten times the size of Britain, a fifth of all Canada. How do you measure the space between a shift in cultural conversation and a landmass three times the size of Texas? What bridges the space between that hope and that realization? What is the scale of the imagination and of the will? What sustained the people whose uncountable small acts shifted the world, since almost no such act has a reward in itself, or soon, or certainly? From what vantage point can you see such incremental, such incomplete, but such extraordinary transformation? These are the parallel narratives to what was going on while neoliberalism and neoconservatism were clambering to their perches of power, and these are evidence of the power that culture has to shape politics, for these profound changes came about as much through changed knowledge and imagination as by legislation. Or, rather, the legislation only came about when the powers that be found this other version of history and of justice irresistible.

The resurgence of the indigenous peoples of the Americas means many things. One is that there are usually cracks somewhere in the inevitable and the obvious. Another is that capitalism and state socialism do not define the range of possibilities, for the indigenous nations often represent significantly different ways of imagining and administrating social and economic systems as well as of connecting spirituality to politics. Relegated to history's graveyard, they have, as have the Zapatistas, inspired the birth of another future. "Another world is possible" has become a rallying cry, and in some ways this is their world, the other future drawn from another past recovered despite everything. This resurgence also demonstrates the sidelong ways of change: from an argument in Geneva to a land mass in northern Canada, from a critique of the past to a new path into the future, from ideas and words to land and power. This is how history is made, out of such unlikely materials, and of hope.

20

Doubt

But the ice on Ellesmere Island at the heart of Nunavut is melting and polar bears are in grave trouble, for their hunting is dependent on summer ice, and chemical contamination is turning some of them into hermaphrodites. There are no words in the Native languages for the new birds arriving in the warming far North, and the Inuit are preparing a lawsuit against the chief perpetrators of climate change. Chunks of the Antarctic ice shelf the size of small European nations are falling into the sea, which is rising enough to threaten the very existence of some of the small islands in the world and the cultures of those islands. Climate change is killing far more people than terrorism. There are nightmarish things at large, and it is not my purpose to deny them. What are the grounds for hope in this world of wrecks?

The United States is the most disproportionate producer of climate change, governed by the most disregardful administration. This country often seems like a train heading for a wreck, with a gullible, apolitical, easily distracted population bloating itself on television's political distortions and repellent vision of human life, with the runaway rates of consumption, the violent interventions around the world, the malignancy of domestic fundamentalism, the burgeoning prison and impoverished and unhinged populations, the decay of democracy, and on and on. It's hard to see radical change in the United States, and easy to see how necessary it is. I spend a lot of time looking at my country in horror.

And a lot of time saying "But" . . . But some plants die from the center and grow outward; the official United States seems like the rotten center of a flourishing world, for elsewhere, particularly around the edges, and even in the margins of this country, beautiful insurrections are flowering. American electoral politics is not the most hopeful direction to look in, and yet the very disastrousness seems sometimes to offer possibility. The Bush administration seems to be doing what every previous administration was too prudent to do: pursuing its unenlightened self-interest so recklessly that it is undermining US standing in the world and the economy that underwrote that standing. The great peace march of February 15, 2003, was a sort of global "fuck you" to that administration, as was the UN Security Council's refusal to endorse the war in Iraq a month later, as was the resistance in Cancun (and at the next staging ground for the US government's globalization agenda, the November 2003 Free Trade Area of the Americas conference in Miami, where the agreements were all postponed or defanged). This won't yield any rapid results, but like polar ice, the old alignments are falling apart, and this time the breakup is liberatory, a birth into the utter unknown of a brave new world.

And this very unknown gives me hope. "The future is dark, which is on the whole, the best thing the future can be, I think," said Virginia Woolf in the midst of the First World War, a war in which millions of young men died horribly. They died, but not everything did. Woolf committed suicide during the next war, but before that she created a body of work of extraordinary beauty and power, power put to use by women to liberate themselves in the years after Woolf was gone, beauty still setting minds on fire.

For many years, one of the great annual sources of gloom has been the Worldwatch Institute's *State of the World* report, but last year's report strikes some startling notes. In it, the aptly named Chris Bright writes,

> But the biggest obstacle to reinventing ourselves may be simply a kind of paralysis of hope. It is possible to see very clearly that our current economies are toxic, destructive on a gargantuan scale, and grossly unfair—to see all this and still have difficulty imagining effective reform . . . We are used to constant flux in the daily details of existence, yet the basic structure of the status quo always looks so unalterable. But it's not. Profound change for the better does occur, even though it can be difficult to see because one of the most common effects of success is to be taken for granted. What looks perfectly ordinary after the fact would often have seemed like a miracle before it.

I have been outlining a series of extraordinary changes in my lifetime. Or, in Bright's terms, miracles. And I have tried to outline this vast, inchoate, nameless movement—not a political movement but a global restlessness, a pervasive shift of imagination and desire—that has recently appeared in almost every part of the world. This, I think, has only just begun, and though it has achieved countless small-scale victories around the world, what its creativity and its power will achieve is yet unimaginable. I have harped on the global justice movement, but there are many other phenomena—for example, South Africa's Truth and Reconciliation Commission as an evolution beyond the binary of vengeance versus acquiescence or silence, a model that is being followed elsewhere. An extraordinary imaginative power to reinvent ourselves is at large in the world, though it is hard to say how it will counteract the dead weight of neoliberalism, fundamentalisms, environmental destructions, and well-marketed mindlessness. But hope is not about what we expect. It is an embrace of the essential unknowability of the world, of the breaks with the present, the surprises. Or perhaps studying the record more carefully leads us to expect miracles—not when and where we expect them, but to expect to be astonished, to expect that we don't know. And this is grounds to act. I believe in hope as an act of defiance, or rather as the foundation for an ongoing series of acts of defiance, those acts necessary to bring about some of what we hope for while we live by principle in the meantime. There is no alternative, except surrender. And surrender not only abandons the future, it abandons the soul.

Subcommandante Marcos says,

> History written by Power taught us that we had lost . . . We did not believe what Power taught us. We skipped class when they taught conformity and idiocy. We failed modernity. We are united by the imagination, by creativity, by tomorrow. In the past we not only met defeat but also found a desire for justice and the dream of being better. We left skepticism hanging from the hook of big capital and discovered that we could believe, that it was worth believing, that we should believe—in ourselves. Health to you, and don't forget that flowers, like hope, are harvested.

And they grow in the dark. "I believe," adds Thoreau, "in the forest, and the meadow, and the night in which the corn grows."

21

Journey to the Center
of the World

The future is dark, but begin in the present, at the Pacific where it fronts my city, where western civilization comes to an end in a strip of sand and the realm of whales and sharks begins. Fish populations are plummeting in this and other oceans, but if you go down the coast a little you'll come to where the sea otters hunted nearly into extinction have come back to the kelp beds, if you go either north or south, you'll come to the beaches where the elephant seals who were likewise nearly exterminated return every winter to fight, mate, and nurse their young. Take a third Pacific species, though, the brown pelican, which also nearly disappeared, then came back, and imagine one pelican's trajectory from Ocean Beach, the western edge of my city and our continent.

Imagine it soaring with the heavy prehistoric grace of a pterodactyl down Fulton Street, the long street that starts at the beach, parallels the north side of Golden Gate Park and carries on after the park ends to run east through the old African American neighborhood, past surviving gospel churches and extinct barbershops to the little formal garden between the War Memorial Building and the Opera House, then straight into City Hall, whose great gilded dome straddles the street (and where four thousand same-sex couples got married in early 2004). Let that pelican soar through the echoing central atrium, where in 1961 students who protested the anticommunist purges were washed down the marble stairs with firehoses, let the bird float out the other side, going on east, to United Nations Plaza, where Fulton dead-ends into Market Street, the city's main artery. This is the place where I stand in the present to face past and future, the place where stories come together, one of the countless centers of the world.

Just before the plaza is the Lick Monument, a colossal Victorian confection of statuary, bas-reliefs, and patriotic inscriptions summing up California history as it looked then. From the west, California as a fierce goddess confronts you, at her feet stands the California Grizzly, extinct everywhere but art and the state flag. Dedicated on Thanksgiving 1894, the monument survived the 1906 earthquake while all the buildings around it crumbled and burned, and it was relocated when the new library opened almost a decade ago. During its relocation a few Native Americans denounced one of its life-size sculptural groupings, the one that shows a Mexican vaquero and padre looming ominously over a prone and apparently conquered Indian. They didn't succeed in getting the statue removed, but they stirred up a furious public conversation about California history, and they won an addition, a bronze plaque below the sculptural group that speaks of genocide and colonialism, a small rewriting of history, a small measure of change.

To the south of the monument is the new public library, built on the site of the sandlot riots of 1877. The sandlot was a space for free speech, but in 1877 the speech turned sordid, incitation to assault and arson against the Chinese population, a degeneration of the great anti-railroad riots that spread across the country that summer when the United States came as close as it ever would to a full-fledged class war. But immediately to the north, staring down the old sandlot, is the superb new Asian Art Museum, a kind of redress or at least an address of the changing status of Asians in this part of America.

Across the street in the plaza proper is a bronze Simón Bolívar, the liberator of South America, on his rearing horse, sometimes with seagulls on his head, one day a year with a group of South American men leaving flowers as tribute. The plaza over whose western end Bolivar presides commemorates the 1945 founding of the United Nations a few blocks away in the War Memorial Building. Huge gold letters in the pavement spell out the preamble of the founding charter. "We the Peoples of the United Nations determined to save succeeding generations from the scourge of war . . . to reaffirm faith in fundamental human rights, in the dignity and worth of the human person, in the equal rights of men and women and of nations large and small," it begins. Two colonnades of stone pillar streetlights are inscribed with the names of the member nations and the year they joined. There's a sort of secret dialogue among these monuments, a conversation about liberation, about imperfect solutions and unfinished revolutions, but still, liberation. And there's more literal sustenance here too.

Every Wednesday and Sunday the plaza hosts a farmers' market, not one of the fancy boutique markets, but a big spread full of affordable food eagerly bought by the poor here in the supermarketless inner city, food grown and sold by Laotians, Latinos, old-time local whites, a small pragmatic United Nations of food production and urban–rural rendezvous. On those days the place is bustling, vibrant, full of the colors of roses, cherries, violet-and-lavender Chinese eggplant, honey, carrots, peppers, sunflowers, and many green things, full of people swinging bags of produce, haggling, hawking, greeting, walking over the words of the UN Charter.

The rest of the time it mostly belongs to the homeless, and so I go once a week to buy food from farmers and once a week to give it away to the destitute. Tuesdays I come here with a young monk from San Francisco Zen Center to feed the people who sit at Bolivar's feet, on the edges of the raised plant beds here and in the grimy surrounding streets. Sometimes the grander political causes are so abstract, so removed, it seems right instead to cook hot food, box it up in Chinese takeout cartons, and give out meals to fifty or sixty people. It's hard to say what difference we make, but we meet people who are hungry, people who bless us, and people who turn away because they're busy shooting up, or crack has taken away their appetites, or suffering has driven them mad. Few remember that there was no significant US homeless population before the 1980s, that Ronald Reagan's new society and economy created these swollen ranks of street people.

Even from City Hall you can see the huge letters of the artist Rigo 23's black, white, and silver mural across Market Street from UN Plaza, the letters that spell out TRUTH, and TRUTH is the far side of this constellation of histories. Rigo dedicated the mural to the Angola Three, the African American political prisoners in Louisiana's Angola Prison. One of them was there for the dedication ceremony, Robert King Wilkerson, a soft-spoken man who spent twenty-nine years in solitary confinement for a murder he did not commit. He was framed for his political activism, then freed in 2001 thanks to the toil of volunteer lawyers who are still working on the cases of the other two.[5] A lot of the marches and demonstrations in San Francisco begin or end here, and so I've been here again and again for peace and justice as well as to get food and to give it away. This is what the world looks like to me, like UN Plaza, full of half-forgotten victories and new catastrophes, of farmers and junkies, of mountains of apples and of people trying to change the world and tell the truth. Someday all this may be ruins over which pelicans will fly, but for now it is a place where history is still unfolding. Today is also the day of creation.

5. Herman Wallace was released in 2013, shortly before his death; Albert Woodfox has seen numerous appeals and a direct order for his immediate release on June 8, 2015, overturned. Robert King Wilkerson now goes by Robert Hillary King. The mural is still there.

Looking Backward

The Extraordinary Achievements of Ordinary People (2009)

Several years ago, 2,600 people lost their lives in Manhattan, and then several million people lost their story. The al-Qaeda attack on the Twin Towers did not defeat New Yorkers. It destroyed the buildings, contaminated the region, killed thousands, and disrupted the global economy, but it most assuredly did not conquer the citizenry. They were only defeated when their resilience was stolen from them by clichés, by the invisibility of what they accomplished that extraordinary morning, and by the very word "terrorism," which suggests that they, or we, were all terrified. The distortion, even obliteration, of what actually happened was a necessary precursor to launching the obscene response that culminated in a war on Iraq, a war we lost (even if some of us don't know that yet), and the loss of civil liberties and democratic principles that went with it.

Only We Can Terrorize Ourselves

Let's remember what actually happened:

When the planes became missiles and the towers became torches and then shards and clouds of dust, many were afraid, but few if any panicked, other than the president, who was far away from danger. The military failed to respond promptly, even though the Pentagon itself was attacked, and the only direct resistance that day came from inside Flight 93, which went down in a field in Pennsylvania on its way to Washington.

Flights 11 and 175 struck the towers. Hundreds of thousands of people rescued each other and themselves, evacuating the buildings and the area, helped in the first minutes, then hours, by those around them. Both PS 150, an elementary school, and the High School for Leadership and Public Service were successfully evacuated—without casualties. In many cases, teachers took students home with them.

A spontaneously assembled flotilla of boats, ranging from a yacht appropriated by policemen to a historic fireboat, evacuated 300,000 to 500,000 people from Lower Manhattan, a nautical feat on the scale of the British evacuation of an army from Dunkirk in the early days of the Second World War; the fleet, that is, rescued in a few hours as many people as the British fleet rescued in days (under German fire admittedly, but then New York's ferry operators and pleasure-boat captains were steering into that toxic cloud on a day when many thought more violence was to come).

Adam Mayblum, who walked down from the eighty-seventh floor of the north tower with some of his coworkers, wrote on the Internet immediately afterward: "They failed in terrorizing us. We were calm. If you want to kill us, leave us alone because we will do it by ourselves. If you want to make us stronger, attack and we unite. This is the ultimate failure of terrorism against the United States."

We failed, however, when we let our own government and media do what that small band from the other side of the earth could not.

Some of us failed, that is, for there were many kinds of response, and some became more radical, more committed, more educated. Mark Fichtel, the president of the New York Coffee, Sugar, and Cocoa Exchange, who scraped his knees badly that morning of September 11 when he was knocked over in a fleeing crowd, was helped to his feet by "a little old lady." He nonetheless had his exchange up and running the next day, and six months later quit his job, began studying Islam, and then teaching about it.

Principal Ada Rosario-Dolch, who on the morning of September 11 set aside concern for her sister Wendy Alice Rosario Wakeford (who died in the towers) to evacuate her high school two blocks away, went to Afghanistan in 2004 to dedicate a school in Herat, Afghanistan, that included a garden memorializing Wakeford.

In a Dust Storm of Altruism

Hollywood movies and too many government pandemic plans still presume that most of us are cowards or brutes, that we panic, trample each other, rampage, or freeze helplessly in moments of crisis and chaos. Most of us believe this, even though it is a slander against the species, an obliteration of what actually happens, and a crippling blow to our ability to prepare for disasters.

Hollywood likes this view because it paves the way for movies starring some superman in the foreground and hordes of stampeding, screaming extras. Without stupid, helpless people to save, heroes become unnecessary. Or rather, without them, it turns out that we are all heroes, even if distinctly unstereotypical ones like that elderly woman who got Fichtel back on his feet. Governments like the grim view for a similar reason: it justifies their existence as repressive, controlling, hostile forces, rather than collaborators with brave and powerful citizenries.

Far more people could have died on September 11 if New Yorkers had not remained calm, had not helped each other out of the endangered buildings and the devastated area, had not reached out to pull people from the collapsing buildings and the dust cloud. The population of the towers was lower than usual that morning, because it was an election day and many were voting before heading to work; it seems emblematic that so many were spared because they were exercising their democratic powers. Others exercised their empathy and altruism. In the evacuation of the towers, John Abruzzo, a paraplegic accountant, was carried down sixty-nine flights of stairs by his coworkers.

Here's how John Guilfoy, a young man who'd been a college athlete, recalled the 9/11 evacuation:

> I remember looking back as I started running, and the thickest smoke was right where it was, you know, a few blocks away, and thinking that, like, whoever's going to be in that is just going to die. There's no way you could—you're going to suffocate, and it was coming at us. I remember just running, people screaming. I was somewhat calm, and I was little bit faster than my colleagues, so I had to stop and slow up a little bit and wait for them to make sure we didn't lose each other.

Had he been in a disaster movie, he would have been struggling in some selfish, social-darwinist way to survive at others' expense, or he would simply have panicked, as we are all supposed to do in disaster. In the reality of September 11, in a moment of supreme danger, he slowed down out of solidarity.

Many New Yorkers that day committed similar feats of solidarity at great risk. In fact, in all the hundreds of oral histories I read and the many interviews I conducted to research my book, *A Paradise Built in Hell*, I could find no one saying he or she was abandoned or attacked in that great exodus. People were frightened and moving fast, but not in a panic. Careful research has led disaster sociologists to the discovery—one of their many counterstereotypical conclusions—that panic is a vanishingly rare phenomenon in disasters, part of an elaborate mythology of our weakness.

A young man from Pakistan, Usman Farman, told of how he fell down and a Hasidic Jewish man stopped, looked at his pendant's Arabic inscription, and then, "with a deep Brooklyn accent he said, 'Brother if you don't mind, there is a cloud of glass coming at us. Grab my hand, let's get the hell out of here.' He was the last person I would ever have thought to help me. If it weren't for him I probably would have been engulfed in shattered glass and debris." A blind newspaper vendor was walked to safety by two women, and a third escorted her to her home in the Bronx.

Errol Anderson, a recruiter with the fire department, was caught outside in that dust storm.

> For a couple of minutes I heard nothing. I thought I was either dead and was in another world, or I was the only one alive. I became nervous and panicky, not knowing what to do, because I couldn't see . . . About four or five minutes later, while I was still trying to find my way around, I heard the voice of a young lady. She was crying and saying, "Please, Lord, don't let me die. Don't let me die." I was so happy to hear this lady's voice. I said, "Keep talking, keep talking, I'm a firefighter, I'll find you by the response of where you are." Eventually we met up with each other and basically we ran into each other's arms without even knowing it.

She held onto his belt and eventually several other people joined them to form a human chain. He helped get them to the Brooklyn Bridge before returning to the site of the collapsed buildings. That bridge became a pedestrian escape route for tens of thousands. For hours, a river of people poured across it. On the far side, Hasidic Jews handed out bottles of water to the refugees. Hordes of volunteers from the region, and within days the nation, converged on Lower

Manhattan, offering to weld, dig, nurse, cook, clean, hear confessions, listen—and did all of those things.

New Yorkers triumphed on that day eight years ago. They triumphed in calm, in strength, in generosity, in improvisation, in kindness. Nor was this something specific to that time or place: San Franciscans during the great earthquake of 1906, Londoners during the Blitz in the Second World War, the great majority of New Orleanians after Hurricane Katrina hit, in fact most people in most disasters in most places have behaved with just this sort of grace and dignity.

It Could Have Been Different

Imagine what else could have sprung from that morning eight years ago. Imagine if the collapse of those towers had not been followed by such a blast of stereotypes, lies, distortions, and fear propaganda that served the agenda of the Bush administration while harming the rest of us—Americans, Iraqis, Afghans, and so many others, for people from ninety nations died in the attacks that day and probably those from many more nations survived at what came to be called Ground Zero.

Not long ago I talked to Roberto Sifuentes, a Chicano performance artist who was then living in New York. Like many New Yorkers, he still marvels at that brief, almost utopian moment of opening in the midst of tragedy, when everyone wanted to talk about meaning, about foreign policy, about history, and did so in public with strangers. It was a moment of passionate engagement with the biggest questions and with one another. On a few occasions, Sifuentes was threatened and nearly attacked for having approximately the same skin tone as an Arab, but he was also moved by the tremendous opening of that moment, the great public dialogue that had begun, and he took part in it with joy.

In five years of investigation and in my own encounter with the San Francisco Bay Area's Loma Prieta earthquake twenty years ago, I've found that disasters are often moments of strange joy. My friend Kate Joyce, then a nineteen-year-old living in New Mexico, had landed in New York on the very morning of September 11, 2001, and spent the next several days in Union Square, the park-like plaza at 14th Street that became a regular gathering point.

She relished the astonishing forum that Union Square became in those days when we had a more perfect union: "We spoke passionately of the contemporary and historical conflicts, contradictions and connections affecting our lives," she wrote me later. "We stayed for hours, through the night, and into the week riveted and expressive, in mourning and humbled, and in the ecstasy of a transformative present." Such conversations took place everywhere.

We had that more perfect union, and then we let them steal it.

Many were killed or widowed or orphaned on that September 11, but none were defeated. Not that day. To remain undefeated we would have had to recognize that such events are immeasurably terrible, but neither so rare as we Americans like to imagine, nor insurmountable. (Since 9/11, far more have been killed in the 2004 Indian Ocean tsunami, the 2005 Pakistan earthquake, the 2008 Burma typhoon, and of course the wars in Afghanistan, Iraq, and the Congo, among other events. More in this country have died of domestic violence since that day.)

After the 9/11 storm struck, the affected civilians in New York were seen as victims; four years later, after Katrina, those in New Orleans were portrayed as brutes. In both cities, the great majority of affected people were actually neither helpless nor savage; they were something else—they were citizens, if by that word we mean civic engagement rather than citizenship status. In both places ordinary people were extraordinarily resourceful, generous, and kind, as were some police officers, firefighters, rescue workers, and a very few politicians. In both cases, the majority of politicians led us astray. All I would have wanted in that September moment, though, was politicians who stayed out of the way, and people who were more suspicious of the news and the newsmakers.

The media, too, stepped between us and the event, failing us with their stock of clichés about war and heroes, their ready adoption of the delusional notion of a "War on Terror," their refusal to challenge the administration as it claimed that somehow the Saudi-spawned, fundamentalist al-Qaeda was linked to the secularist Iraqi government of Saddam Hussein and that we should fear mythical Iraqi "weapons of mass destruction." Rarely did they mention that we had, in fact, been bombing Iraq without interruption since 1991.

After 9/11, it could all have been different, profoundly different. And if it had, there would have been no children imprisoned without charges or release dates in our gulag in Cuba; there would have been no unmanned drones slaughtering wedding parties in the rural backlands of Afghanistan or the Iraqi desert; there would have been no soldiers returning to the United States with two or three limbs missing or their heads and minds grievously damaged (there were already 320,000 traumatic brain injuries to soldiers deployed to Iraq and Afghanistan by early 2008, according to the RAND Corporation); there would not have been a next round of American deaths—4,334 in Iraq, 786 in Afghanistan to date; there would have been no trillion dollars taken from constructive projects to fatten the corporations of war; no extreme corrosion of the Bill of Rights, no usurpation of powers by the executive branch. Perhaps.

We Are the Monument

It could all have been different. It's too late now, but not too late, never too late, to change how we remember and commemorate this event and that other great landmark of the Bush era, Hurricane Katrina, and so prepare for disasters to come.

For the ninety-nine years before that hurricane hit the Gulf Coast on August 29, 2005, the biggest urban disaster in American history was in my city, San Francisco. Half the city, including more than 28,000 buildings, was destroyed, and about 3,000 people probably died. The earthquake early on the morning of April 18, 1906, did a lot of damage, but the fires did more. Some were started by collapsed buildings and broken gas mains, others by the army troops who streamed in from the Presidio at the northern tip of the city and ineptly built firebreaks that instead actually spread the fires.

The presiding officer, Brigadier General Frederick Funston, presumed that the public would immediately revert to chaos and that his task was restoring order. In the first days after the disaster, the truth was more or less the other way around, as the army and the National Guard prevented citizens from fighting the fires and collecting their property, shot people as looters (including rescuers and bystanders), and generally regarded the public as the enemy (as did some of the officials presiding over the post-Katrina "rescue"). As with many disasters, a calamity that came from outside was magnified by elite fears and institutional failures within. Still, on their own, San Franciscans organized themselves remarkably, fought fires when they could, created a plethora of community kitchens, helped reconnect separated families, and began to rebuild.

Every year we still celebrate the anniversary of the earthquake at Lotta's Fountain, which, like Union Square after 9/11, became a meeting place for San Franciscans in the largely ruined downtown. That gathering brings hundreds of people together before dawn to sing the silly song "San Francisco," get free whistles from the Red Cross, and pay homage to the dwindling group of survivors.

San Francisco now uses the anniversary to put out the message that we should be prepared for the next disaster—not the version the Department of Homeland Security spread in the years after 9/11 with the notion that preparation consists of fear, duct tape, deference, and more fear, but practical stuff about supplies and strategies. My city even trains anyone who wants to become a certified NERT—for the nerdy-sounding Neighborhood Emergency Response Team—member, and about seventeen thousand of us are badge-carrying, hard hat–owning NERT members (including me).

Every city that has had, or will have, a disaster should have such a carnival of remembrance and preparation. For one thing, it commemorates all the ways that San Franciscans were not defeated and are not helpless; for another, it reminds us that, in disaster, we are often at our best, however briefly, that in those hours and days many have their best taste of community, purposefulness, and power. (Reason enough for many of those who are supposed to be in charge to shudder.) For the fourth anniversary of Hurricane Katrina, New Orleanians were invited to ring bells, lay wreaths, pray, encircle the Superdome—that miserable shelter of last resort for those stranded in the hurricane and flood—and, of course, listen to music and dance in the streets to second-line parades, but also to keep volunteering and rebuilding. (Perhaps the most overlooked aspect of that disaster is the vast army of citizen volunteers who came to the city's aid, when the government didn't, and are still doing so.)

New York has its pillars of light and readings of names for the anniversary of 9/11, but it seems to lack any invitation to the citizenry to feel its own power and prepare for the next calamity.[6] For there will be next times for San Francisco, New York, New Orleans, and possibly—in

---

6. This was, of course, written before Hurricane Sandy, when many New Yorkers did a remarkable job of responding to the aftermath. Many of them came from networks created during Occupy Wall Street, and some of the spirit and tactics of that movement were carried over (so that anti-authoritarianism wasn't only present but essential to the framework of do-it-yourself mutual aid that prevailed). The alliances formed with community organizations, religious centers, and neighborhood groups lasted and branched out into some long-term projects and alliances.

this era of extreme and turbulent weather, and economic upheaval—a great many other cities and towns in this country and elsewhere.

The rebuilt city, the eventual rise of disaster preparedness, the people who go on with their everyday lives—these are the monument San Francisco needed and every city needs to transcend its calamities. New Yorkers could gather in Union Square and elsewhere to remember what happened, really remember, remember that the heroes weren't necessarily men, or in uniform, but were almost everyone everywhere that day.

They could open their hearts and minds to discuss mourning, joy, death, violence, power, weakness, truth and lies, as they did that week. They could consider what constitutes safety and security, what else this country could be, and what its foreign and energy policies have to do with these things. They could walk the streets together to demonstrate that New York is still a great city, whose people were not frightened into going into hiding or flight from public and urban life. They could more consciously and ceremoniously do what New Yorkers, perhaps best of all Americans, do every day: coexist boldly and openly in a great mixture of colors, nationalities, classes, and opinions, daring to speak to strangers and to live in public.

The dead must be remembered, but the living are the monument, the living who coexist in peace in ordinary times and who save one another in extraordinary times. Civil society triumphed that morning in full glory. Look at it: remember that this is who we were and can be.

Everything's Coming Together While Everything Falls Apart (2014)

The most thrilling bureaucratic document I've ever seen was exciting for exactly one reason: it was dated the twenty-first day of the month of Thermidor in the Year Six. Written in sepia ink on heavy paper, it documented a land auction in the center of France in what we would call late summer 1798. But the date written on the first page meant that the document was created when the French Revolution was the overarching reality of an everyday life in which things as fundamental as the distribution of power and the nature of government had been reborn in astonishing ways. In 1792, a new calendar starting with the Year One was created to start society itself over again.

In the little junk shop on a quiet street in San Francisco, I held a relic from inside one of the great upheavals of the last millennium. It made me think of a remarkable statement by the great feminist fantasy writer Ursula K. LeGuin a few weeks earlier. In the course of an awards speech she noted, "We live in capitalism. Its power seems inescapable. So did the divine right of kings. Any human power can be resisted and changed by human beings." The document I purchased for five dollars was written a few years after the French got over the idea that the divine right of kings was inescapable, executed their king for his crimes, and tried out some other forms of government. It's popular to say the experiment failed, but France never regressed to absolutist monarchy or the belief in its legitimacy, and its experiments inspired other liberatory movements around the world (and terrified monarchs and aristocrats).[7]

Americans are good at the mingled complacency and despair that says things cannot change, will not change, and we do not have power to change them. You'd have to be an amnesiac or at least ignorant of history and even current events to fail to see that our country and our world have always been changing, are in the midst of great and terrible changes, and are occasionally changed through the power of the popular will and idealistic movements. Climate now demands we summon

---

7. David Graeber writes in a 2013 essay, "Already by the time of the French Revolution, [Immanuel] Wallerstein notes, there was a single world market, and increasingly a single world political system as well, dominated by the huge colonial empires. As a result, the storming of the Bastille in Paris could well end up having effects on Denmark, or even Egypt, just as profound as on France itself—in some cases, even more so. Hence he speaks of the 'world revolution of 1789,' followed by the 'world revolution of 1848,' which saw revolutions break out almost simultaneously in fifty countries, from Wallachia to Brazil. In no case did the revolutionaries succeed in taking power, but afterward, institutions inspired by the French Revolution—notably, universal systems of primary education—were put in place pretty much everywhere. Similarly, the Russian Revolution of 1917 was a world revolution ultimately responsible for the New Deal and European welfare states as much as for Soviet communism. The last in the series was the world revolution of 1968—which, much like 1848, broke out almost everywhere, from China to Mexico, seized power nowhere, but nonetheless changed everything. This was a revolution against state bureaucracies, and for the inseparability of personal and political liberation, whose most lasting legacy will likely be the birth of modern feminism."

up the force to leave behind the Age of Fossil Fuel (and maybe with it some of the Age of Capitalism).

How to Topple a Giant

To use Le Guin's language, physics is inevitable: if you put more carbon dioxide into the atmosphere, the planet warms, and as the planet warms, various kinds of chaos and ruin are loosed. Politics, on the other hand, is not inevitable. For example, not so many years ago it would have seemed inevitable that Chevron Corporation, currently the third biggest corporation in the country, would run the refinery town of Richmond, California, as its own private fiefdom. You could say that the divine right of Chevron seemed inevitable. Except that people refused to believe that, and this town of 107,000 mostly poor nonwhite people pushed back.

In recent years, a group of progressives won election to the city council and mayor's seat, despite huge expenditures by Chevron, the corporation that also brought you gigantic oil spills onshore in Ecuador and offshore in Brazil, an oil platform explosion off the coast of Nigeria, and Canadian tar-sands bitumen sent by rail to the Richmond refinery. Mayor Gayle McLaughlin and the others had a little revolution in a town that had mostly been famous for its crime rate and for Chevron's toxic refinery emissions, which periodically create emergencies requiring everyone to shelter in place (and pretend that they were not being poisoned indoors).

As McLaughlin put it, in her era as mayor,

> We've accomplished so much, including breathing better air, reducing the pollution and building a cleaner environment and cleaner jobs, and reducing our crime rate. Our homicide number is the lowest in thirty-three years and we became a leading city in the Bay Area for solar installed per capita. We're a sanctuary city. And we're defending our homeowners to prevent foreclosures

and evictions. And we also got Chevron to pay $114 million extra dollars in taxes.

For the November 2014 election, the second-largest oil company on earth officially spent $3.1 million to defeat McLaughlin and other progressive candidates and instate its own. The sum works out to $180 per voter, but my brother David, who's long been involved in Richmond politics, points out that if you look at all the other ways they spend to influence local politics, it might be ten times that. Chevron lost. None of its candidates were elected, and all the grassroots progressives it fought with billboards, mailers, television ads, websites, and everything else the lavishly funded smear campaign could think of, won.

If a small grassroots coalition can win locally against a corporation valued at $228.9 billion, a global coalition could win against the fossil-fuel giants. It wasn't easy in Richmond; it won't be easy on the largest scale, but it's not impossible, either. Richmond progressives won by imagining that the status quo was not inevitable or eternal and showing up to do the work to make it so. The billionaires and the fossil-fuel corporations are intensely engaged in politics and count on us staying on the sidelines. If you look at their response to various movements you can see that they are afraid of us, if we wake up, if we show up, if we exercise our power to counter theirs.

We need to end the age of fossil fuel the way the French ended the age of absolute monarchy. We can't say it's impossible, or possible, and what is possible has been changing rapidly.

Three Kinds of Hero

If you look at the energy-technology engineers—and this may be an era in which engineers are our unsung heroes—the future is tremendously exciting. Not very long ago the climate movement was only hoping technology could save us; now, as one of the six great banners carried in the four-hundred-thousand-strong September 21, 2014, climate march said, "We have the solutions." Wind and solar and other technologies are spreading rapidly, with better designs, lower costs, and many extraordinary improvements that will, undoubtedly, continue for some time.

Clean energy is in many parts of the country and the world cheaper than fossil fuel (though the sudden drop in oil prices may scramble that for a little while, but has the nice side effect of pushing some of the more farfetched and filthy extraction schemes below the cost-effective point for now). The technology has gotten so much better, cheaper, and more widespread that sober financial advisors are calling fossil fuels and centralized conventional power plants a bad investment and talking about the carbon bubble (which is a sign that the divestment movement has worked in calling attention to the practical as well as the moral problems of the industry). The technology front is encouraging.

That's the carrot for action; there's also a stick.

If you listen to the scientists—and scientists are another set of heroes for our time—the news keeps getting scarier. You probably know already know the highlights: chaotic weather, broken weather records, this year's several hottest months on record, 355 months in a row of above-average temperatures, more ice melting, more ocean acidification, extinction, the spread of tropical diseases, drop in food productivity with consequent famines. So many people don't grasp what we're up against, because they don't think about Earth and its systems much or they don't grasp the delicate, intricate reciprocities and counterbalances that keep it all running as well as it has since the last ice age ended and an abundant, calm Earth emerged. It's not real or vivid or visceral or even visible for most of us.

It is for a great many scientists whose fields have something to do with climate. In many cases they're scared, they're sad, and they're clear about the urgency of taking action to limit how disastrous climate change is for our species and for the systems we depend upon.

Many people outside the loop think that it's too late to do anything, which, as premature despair always does, excuses us for doing nothing. Though there are diverse opinions quite a lot of insiders think that what we do now matters tremendously, because the difference between the best and worst case scenarios is vast, and the future is not yet written.

After that four-hundred-thousand-person-strong climate march in September of 2014, I asked my friend Jamie Henn, a cofounder of and communications director for 350.org, how he viewed this moment, and he said, "Everything's coming together while everything's falling apart," a beautiful summary of the heartening engineering and activist news in the shadow of the terrible scientific reports. This brings us to the third group of heroes, the one that, unlike science and engineering, doesn't require special qualifications: activists.

The new technologies are only solutions if they're implemented and the old ones—the carbon-emitting ones—are phased out or shut down. We need to keep the great majority of fossil fuel in the ground and move away from the Age of Petroleum. That's the conclusion of a relatively recent calculation made by scientists and publicized and pushed by activists (and maybe made conceivable by engineers designing replacement systems). The goal is to keep warming to 2 degrees Celsius (3.5 degrees Fahrenheit), and even that goal, established years ago, is being questioned as too lenient by scientists alarmed by what 1 degree Celsius of warming is already doing and will continue to do.

Dismantling the fossil-fuel economy might have the nice side effect of dismantling a lot of the warping power that oil has had in global and national politics. Of course those wielding that power will not yield it without a ferocious battle—and that is the very battle the climate movement is engaged in now, on many fronts, from the divestment movement to the fight against fracking to the endeavor to stop the Keystone XL pipeline and others like it, from the tar sands to the quite successful movement to shut down coal-fired power plants in the United States and prevent others from being built.

What Did You Do During the War?

If everyone who's passionate about climate, who truly gets that we're living in a pivotal moment, found their place in the movement, amazing things could happen. What's happening now is already remarkable, if not yet adequate to the crisis. A few years ago there was no fossil-fuel divestment movement; it is now active on hundreds of college campuses and at other institutions, and while the intransigence of bureaucracy remains a remarkable force, there have been notable victories. The Rockefeller Foundation—made fat upon the wealth of John D. Rockefeller's founding role in the rise of the petroleum industry—pledged to divest their $860 million in assets from fossil fuels in late September, one of more than eight hundred institutions—church denominations, universities, cities, pension funds, foundations—to commit to do so globally so far, from Scotland to New Zealand to Seattle.[8]

The KXL pipeline could have been up and running years ago with little fanfare had activists not taken it on.[9] It became a profoundly public, hotly debated issue, the subject of demonstrations at nearly every presidential appearance in recent years. In the course of this ruckus, a great many people (including me) were clued into the existence of the giant suppurating sore of sludge, bitumen, and poison lakes that is the Alberta Tar Sands. Canadians, particularly indigenous Canadians

---

8. More than $3.4 trillion was divested or committed to divestment from fossil fuels by the end of 2015.

9. In early November 2015, Obama vetoed plans for the northern stretch of the KXL pipeline, a huge victory for the climate movement after six years of presidential waffling and activist campaigning.

in surrounding regions, have done a remarkable job of blocking other pipelines to keep this landlocked stuff from reaching any coast for refining and export. Some of it is now shipped by rail, but trains cost significantly more than pipelines, and, with the dramatic drop in the price of oil, lack of pipelines means a lack of profit for many of the tarsands projects, effectively cancelling them.

The climate movement has come of age. And it has achieved many things that had been pronounced impossible not long ago. (2016 update: in Canada, newly elected prime minister Justin Trudeau banned oil tankers on the country's northwest coast, effectively killing another oil pipeline route for the Alberta Tar Sands. The news came amid other landmark decisions, including presidential bans on drilling in the Arctic and on new coal leases on public land; a halt to new oil and gas leases in Utah; a ban on new fossil-fuel infrastructure in Portland, Oregon, that may become a model for other local climate legislation; introduction of a Senate bill [presumably doomed but indicative of changing perspectives] to ban all new oil and gas leases on public land and some coastal waters; and two landmark victories in New York State. New York activists, who'd won a historic ban on fracking in that state in 2014, got their governor to veto a natural gas port, and investigative journalism that had led to revelations that Exxon possessed, and suppressed, accurate information about the coming impact of climate change prompted the New York attorney general to issue subpoenas that could lead to a criminal investigation of the world's largest oil corporation.)

Really, the climate movement is bigger and more effective than it looks, because most people don't see a single movement; if they look hard, they see a wildly diverse mix of groups facing global issues on one hand and a host of local ones, such as fracking, on others. Domestically, that can mean the city of Denton, Texas, banning fracking in November 2014 or the amazing work by antifracking activists in New York State, which resulted in a statewide fracking ban, the first of its kind in the United States. It can mean people working on college divestment campaigns or on rewriting state laws to address climate by implementing efficiency and clean energy.

It can mean the British Columbia activists who, for now, prevented a tunnel being drilled for a tar-sands pipeline to the Pacific Coast with a months-long encampment, civil disobedience, and many arrests at Burnaby Mountain, near Vancouver. One of the arrested wrote, in the Vancouver *Observer*, "But sitting in that jail cell, I felt a weight lift from my shoulders. One that I was only partially aware that I have been carrying for years now. I am ashamed by Canada's withdrawal from the Kyoto treaty and our increasingly contemptible position on climate change. If these are the values of our society then I want to be an outlaw in that society."

Making the Future

The climate movement has grown remarkably—but it must grow far more to be adequate to the crisis. Which is where you come in, if you haven't yet. The quiet chorus of the everyday can drown out the voice of history, calling us to action in the moment for the big future. I can barely remember what seemed so pressing when I didn't participate in great historical moments, but I know that the same kind of things seem pressing now, and that I have to push some of them aside.

Just before the climate march I began to contemplate how human beings half a century or a century from now will view us, who lived in the era when climate change was recognized and there was so much that could be done about it, so much more than we have done. They may hate us, despise us, see us as the people who squandered their patrimony, like drunkards gambling away the family fortune that, in this case, is everyone's everywhere and everything, the natural world itself when it was in good working order. They will regard us as people who rearranged the china when the house was on fire.

They will think we were insane to worry about celebrities and fleeting political scandals and whether we had nice bodies; they will think the newspapers should have had a gigantic black box above the fold of the front page every day saying "Here are some stories about other things BUT CLIMATE IS BIGGER THAN THIS" and every news broadcast should have opened with the equivalent. Every day. They will think that we should have thrown our bodies in the way of the engines of destruction, raised our voices to the heavens, stopped everything until the destruction stopped. They will bless and praise the few and curse the many.

There have been heroic people in every country and some remarkable achievements. The movement has grown in size, power, and sophistication, but it needs to grow a lot more to be commensurate to what is required. I realized that this included me and realized that it was time to shift my priorities, to make my mild engagement with climate something larger and fiercer.

This is the time to find your place in it, if you haven't yet. And for the climate organizers to do better at reaching out and offering everyone a part in the transformation, whether it's the housebound person who writes letters or the twenty-year-old who's ready for direct action in remote places. There's a role for everyone, and it's everyone's most important work right now. So many other important matters press upon us—human rights and justice work, the care for the most vulnerable—but it has to be part of what you do. It is the big perspective from which everything else must be seen (and the Philippines' charismatic former climate negotiator Yeb Sano notes, "Climate change impinges on almost all human rights. Human rights are at the core of this issue.")

Many people believe that personal virtue is what matters in this crisis. It's a good thing, but it's not the key thing. It's great to bicycle rather than drive, eat plants instead of animals, put solar panels on your roof, but it can give you a false sense you're not part of the problem. You are not just what you personally do or do not consume but part of a greater problem if you are a citizen of a country that is a major carbon emitter, as is nearly everyone in the English-speaking nations and the global north. You are part of the system, and you need, we all need, to change that system. Nothing less than systemic change will save us.

The race is on. From an ecological standpoint, the scientists advise us that we still have a little bit of time, a closing window, in which it might still be possible, by a swift, decisive move away from fossil fuel in particular, to limit climate change to two degrees Celsius of warming. Which will be considerably less devastating than some of the higher numbers we will slide toward if we don't reverse course.

The pressure on nations comes from within, not from each other. Here in the United States, long the world's biggest carbon-emitter (until China outstripped us, partly by becoming the manufacturer of a high percentage of our products), we have a particular responsibility to push hard. The pressure works. The president is clearly feeling it, and it's reflected in the recent US–China agreement on curtailing emissions—far from perfect or adequate, but a huge step forward.

How will we get to where we need to be? No one knows, but we know that we must keep moving in the direction of reduced carbon emissions, a transformed energy economy, an escape from the tyranny of the oil companies, and a vision of a world in which everything is connected. We need change on a colossal scale, and we don't know if we can achieve that unless we try. The story of this coming year is ours to write, and it could be a story of the Year One in the climate revolution, of the watershed when popular resistance changed the fundamentals as much as the people of France changed their world more than two hundred years ago.

May, two hundred years hence, someone hold a document from 2019 in their hand, in wonder, because it was written when the revolution had taken hold and all the old inevitabilities had been swept aside, when we seized hold of possibility and made it ours. "Any human power can be resisted and changed by human beings," said LeGuin. It's the hardest and the best work we could ever do. Now, everything depends on it.

Backward and Forward

An Afterword

This book was written *for* something—for the encouragement of activists who share some of my dreams and values. We are all activists in some way or another, because our actions (and inactions) have impact. And it was written *against* something—a defeatist, dismissive frame of mind that is far too widespread. We talk about politics as though they were a purely rational exercise in the world of deeds and powers, but how we view that world and act in it has its roots in identities and emotions. There is, in other words, an inner life to politics, and I wanted to get at it, to plant and to weed there.

I went on the road from 2003 onward, talking about hope, change, civil society movements, and the power of stories. I met with joyous embrace of the ideas I was talking about from people who'd already arrived at their own versions of these ideas independently, and from people who wanted encouragement or alternative views. Often, I also encountered bitterness, defeatism, and sometimes rage. It was, at first, surprising that talking about hope made some people furious.

Some had the sense that they were protectors of knowledge that might otherwise be lost, about injustices and wrongs and injuries, and they saw those as the stories that need to be told. I had a different sense, that we need stories that don't gloss over the ugly damage out there but that don't portray it as all there is either. The mainstream media don't tell much about the dank underside of our institutions and the damage they do, but they won't tell you much about populist insurrections, grassroots victories, or beautiful alternatives either. Both matter; because the former are so well attended to, I've taken the latter as my beat.

The despairing were deeply attached to their despair, so much so I came to refer to my project as stealing the teddy bear of despair from the loving arms of the left. What did it give that particular sector of the left? It got them off the hook, for one thing. If the world is totally doomed no matter what, little or nothing is demanded of you in response. You can go be bitter and idle on your sofa if you're already comfortable and safe. It was striking that the people with the most at stake were often the most hopeful. And that those who were active were often hopeful, though it may be the other way around: some of those who are hopeful are active. Yet the range of the hopeful extends beyond that, and you can find hope in surprising corners.

Early in my hope tours, I gave a talk to a roomful of people of color in Washington State. Some had memories of the civil rights movement, some identified with their fellow Mexicans who'd risen up as the Zapatistas, and a small, elegant Asian woman about my age said, in a voice of bell-like clarity, "I think that is right. If I had not hoped, I would not have struggled. And if I had not struggled, I would not have survived Pol Pot." It was a stunning statement, by a Cambodian immigrant whose hope must have been small and narrow at the time—just to survive. I am often amazed at the lack of bitterness on the part of many of those who have most right to it, though I've seen exhaustion, physical, emotional, and moral, among frontline activists.

For the desperate, the alternative to hope—and the struggle to realize that hope—is death or privation or torture or a grim future or no future for their children. They are motivated. From afar I've watched the Coalition of Immokalee Workers, the mostly undocumented Haitian, Latino, and Mayan Indian immigrants who fought for farmworkers' rights with panache, brilliance, and creativity for the last decade. Realizing they couldn't extract a living wage from farmers, they went after the buyers and brought gigantic corporations—McDonald's, Walmart, Burger King, Taco Bell, Whole Foods—into line with their fair-price terms for tomato pickers. Along the way they were cheerful, spirited, and hopeful.

It seemed in part to be a cultural style. There's a romantic idealism in Latin American politics, a sense of possibility for the world and heroic engagement for the self. It may come from recent memories of death squads and beautiful insurrections and from turbulent national histories, from a sense that everything can change suddenly, for the better or the worse. That it's not a problem of the English language is evident in the beautiful spirit of many Black movements past and present, some of them faith-based, some of them energized by hip-hop.

And then there were my people, middle-class white people. It was as though many of us didn't know how to be this other kind of person, this person who could speak of big dreams, of high ideals, of deep emotions, as though something more small-scale and sarcastic was the reduced version of self that remained to us. I've had great visionary companions the past dozen years from many places and races, but I've met so many of my kind who are attached for various reasons to their limits and their misery.

A friend born in the 1950s reminds me that his generation in their youth really expected a revolution—the old kind where people march with weapons and overthrow the government and establish a utopia—and were permanently disappointed that it hadn't come to pass. When I was young, people still jestingly said, "After the revolution," but the catchphrase came from the idea that regime change was how to change everything, and that nothing short of regime change mattered. Though everything had changed—not enough on many fronts, but tremendously. And everything matters. My friend's different from many of his peers, and we talked about the more profound revolutions that had unfolded in our lifetimes, around race, gender, sexuality, food, economics, and so much more, the slow incremental victories that begin in the imagination and change the rules. But seeing those revolutions requires looking for something very different than armed cadres. It also requires being able to recognize the shades of gray between black and white or maybe to see the world in full color.

Much has changed; much needs to change; being able to celebrate or at least recognize milestones and victories and keep working is what the times require of us. Instead, a lot of people seem to be looking for trouble, the trouble that reinforces their dismal worldview. Everything that's not perfect is failed, disappointing, a betrayal. There's idealism in there, but also unrealistic expectations, ones that cannot meet with anything but disappointment. Perfectionists often position themselves on the sidelines, from which they point out that nothing is good enough.

The idea that something is flawed, doomed, fatally compromised, or just no good frequently arises from what I call naïve cynicism. It often comes out of less information and less responsibility for results than deeply engaged activists have. I've often seen, say, a landmark piece of climate legislation hailed as a victory and celebrated by people working hardest on the issue, but dismissed and disparaged by those who are doing little or nothing for the cause in question. They don't actually know what work went into producing the legislation, what it will achieve, and what odds were overcome to get it. Criticizing it seems to be a way of reinforcing an identity, but that criticism is often vague and ill informed when it comes to the facts. And the question arises about that identity too: is it attached to losing? Nevertheless, such dismissive critiques are often presented as worldliness, as knowledge and experience, even when they draw from neither.

The naively cynical measure a piece of legislation, a victory, a milestone not against the past or the limits of the possible but against their ideas of perfection, and as this book reminds you, perfection is a yardstick by which everything falls short. They may fear that celebrating anything means undermining the dissatisfaction that drives us—if dissatisfaction drives us rather than parks us in the parking lot of the disconsolate. The business of how we get from bad to good, from dying to surviving and maybe to thriving, isn't their responsibility. The deeply engaged well know that the particular bit of legislation under discussion isn't everything we hope for, doesn't get us all the way there, and also know that it can be a step forward from which further steps can and must be taken, and that change is often made incrementally, not by a great leap from evil to pure goodness.

Maybe an underlying problem is that despair isn't even an ideological position but a habit and a reflex. I have found, during my adventures in squandering time on social media, that a lot of people respond to almost any achievement, positive development, or outright victory with "yes but." Naysaying becomes a habit. Yes, this completely glorious thing had just happened, but the entity that achieved it had done something bad at another point in history. Yes, the anguish of this group was ended, but somewhere some other perhaps unrelated group was suffering hideously. It boiled down to: we can't talk about good things until there are no more bad things. Which, given that the supply of bad things is inexhaustible, and more bad things are always arising, means that we can't talk about good things at all. Ever.

Sometimes it seemed to come out of a concern that we would abandon the unfinished work if we celebrated, a sense that victories or even joy and confidence are dangerous. That celebrating or just actively fomenting change is dangerous.

The young activist Yotam Marom, who came of age as an activist at Occupy Wall Street, contemplated this state of affairs in the essay "Undoing the Politics of Powerlessness." He wrote:

> Today, when I think about the politics of powerlessness, it feels clear as day to me that the source of all of it is fear. Fear of leaders, of the enemy, of the possibility of having to govern, of the stakes of winning and losing, of each other, of ourselves. And it's all pretty

understandable. We call each other out and push one another out of the movement, because we are desperate to cling to the little slivers of belonging we've found in the movement, and are full of scarcity—convinced that there isn't enough of anything to go around (money, people, power, even love). We eat ourselves alive and attack our own leaders because we've been hurt and misled all our lives and can't bear for it to happen again on our watch ... And perhaps most importantly: Our tendency to make enemies of each other is driven by a deep fear of the real enemy, a paralyzing hopelessness about our possibilities of winning. After all, whether we admit it or not, we spend quite a lot of our time not believing we can really win. And if we're not going to win, we might as well just be awesome instead. If we're not going to win, we're better off creating spaces that suit our cultural and political tastes, building relationships that validate our non-conformist aesthetic, surrendering the struggle over the future in exchange for a small island over which we can reign.

How do we get back to the struggle over the future? I think you have to hope, and hope in this sense is not a prize or a gift, but something you earn through study, through resisting the ease of despair, and through digging tunnels, cutting windows, opening doors, or finding the people who do these things. They exist. "You gotta give them hope," said Harvey Milk long ago, and then he did exactly that.

I believe that you can talk about both the terrible things we should engage with and the losses behind us, as well as the wins and achievements that give us the confidence to endeavor to keep pursuing the possibilities. I write to give aid and comfort to people who feel overwhelmed by the defeatist perspective, to encourage people to stand up and participate, to look forward at what we can do and back at what we have done. This book was always for them. And if you've read this far, for you.

Acknowledgments

This book is one part of a vast, ongoing conversation about who we are, what powers we have, and what we can do with them, and it comes out of readings, conversations, friendships, and organizing with many brilliant, heroic, and kind people over the years, often people who drew me deeper into their part of the world and the work. Especially my brother David; political theorist, idealist, documenter of horizontalidad, dear friend, and inspiration Marina Sitrin; Bob Fulkerson of the Progressive Leadership Alliance of Nevada and Kaitlin Backlund and Jo Anne Garret (1925–2013), whose friendship has been the most direct reward for my years of environmental work in that state; Utah environmental writer Chip Ward; Oklahoma indigenous organizer and longtime friend Pam Kingfisher; John Jordan of Reclaim the Streets in London in the 1990s, now a climate activist in France; nonviolence theorist and writer Jonathan Schell, much missed since his untimely death in 2014; Stephen Zunes and Erica Chenoweth, great and hopeful theorists of nonviolence now; my friends at 350.org Bill McKibben, Payal Parekh, Jamie Henn, Anna Goldstein, and May Boeve; all the great activists of Occupy Wall Street in its many manifestations, especially the brilliant Astra Taylor, now of Strike Debt, who's also a beloved friend; musician, physician, and everyday co-conspirator Rupa Marya; feminist and friend Elena Acevedo Dalcourt and the many feminists whose online discourse has helped refine and shape my ideas about gender and justice; Father Louis Vitale; Zenkei Blanche

Hartman; Guillermo Gomez-Pena; David Graeber; Barry Lopez and Terry Tempest Williams, whose depth in writing and speaking inspired me to go deeper as this book was taking shape; my amazing activist cousins once removed, Mary Solnit Clarke (1916–1997) and June Solnit Sale, founding members of Women Strike for Peace, the latter in her seventh decade of human rights activism; my comrade in hope Sam Green; Brad Erickson, an important early influence on my understanding of indigenous politics; Antonia Juhasz; Maya Gallus; Genine Lentine; Thomas Evans; Gustavo Esteva; Paul Yamazaki; Patrick Marks and Gent Sturgeon; and so many more people that this list could never be completed.

Notes

A Note on Terminology

For people pursuing and supporting liberation, justice, democracy and human rights, there is a cluster of overlapping terms: *left* and *leftist*, *progressive*, and *radical* among them. *Left*, I argue elsewhere in this book, is an outdated term for how the world is divided and carries a lot of baggage; by using it mostly as a pejorative, I pack a little more into it. *Progressive* carries outdated notions of progress with it. And *radical* is often viewed as meaning dangerous, insofar as those willing to consider real change are dangerous.

Like some of my peers I have fallen back on the term *left* to describe the old and somewhat problematic realm from which the activism I support comes—or departs; *radical* is less attached to history and more useful to describe those interested in changing the world, and I will lean on it. The root of the word, *radice*, literally means "root" and suggests that radicals get to the bottom of things, to the causes rather than the effects.

Furthermore, I use the word *activist* as shorthand repeatedly, which overlooks those whose everyday pursuits—schoolteachers, organic farmers—are an activism, but not a confrontational one—and it ignores the other kinds of activists, antifeminists, racists, private-property extremists, who are working against justice, human rights, and so forth. Bear with me until we come up with better language.

Endnotes

Foreword

xxii "The struggle for justice...": Howard Zinn, "The Optimism of Uncertainty," in Zinn, *Failure to Quit: Reflections of an Optimistic Historian* (Monroe, ME: Common Courage Press, 2003).

1: Looking into Darkness

1 Virginia Woolf, "The future is dark . . .": *The Diary of Virginia Woolf*, vol. 1 (New York: Harcourt, 1981).

4 Ernst Bloch, "The work of this emotion" in *The Principle of Hope*, vol. 1, trans., Neville Plaice, Stephen Plaice, and Paul Knight (Cambridge, MA: MIT Press, 1986), 3.

2: When We Lost

8 Eduardo Galeano, "A few days": "Where the People Voted Against Fear," *Progressive*, November 2004.

9 Roger Burbach, "There is indeed a Chilean alternative": "Why They Hate Bush in Chile," *Counterpunch*, November 22, 2004, www.counterpunch. org/2004/11/22/why-they-hate-bush-in-chile.

11 Arundhati Roy, "For many of us": "Darkness Passed," Outlook India, May 14, 2004, http://www.outlookindia.com/full.asp?fodname=20040514&f-name=ro y&sid=1.

11 F. Scott Fitzgerald, "The test of a first-rate," in *The Crack Up* (New York: New Directions, 1956), 69.

11 Vaclav Havel, "The kind of hope I often think about": *Disturbing the Peace: A Conversation with Karel Hvizdala*, trans. and intro. by Paul Wilson (New York: Vintage Books, 1990), 181.

12 Paolo Freire, "Without a minimum of hope": *Pedagogy of Hope: Reliving Pedagogy of the Oppressed* (New York: Continuum Books, 1994), 9.

3: What We Won

16 Gary Younge, "The antiwar movement got the German chancellor": "For Better—or Worse," Guardian, October 6, 2003, www.theguardian.com/politics/2003/oct/06/iraq.iraq.

4: False Hope and Easy Despair

19   Bloch, *Principle of Hope*, 5.

5: A History of Shadows

26   Schell quotes John Adams saying that the American Revolution "was in the minds of the people": Jonathan Schell, *The Unconquerable World: Power, Nonviolence, and the Will of the People* (New York: Metropolitan Books, 2003), 160.

26   "in the new world of politically committed and active people," ibid.

27   He continues, "Individual hearts and minds change," ibid.

27   Adam Hochschild, *Bury the Chains: Prophets and Rebels in the Fight to Free an Empire's Slaves* (New York: Houghton Mifflin, 2005).

32   Chip Ward, *Hope's Horizon: Three Visions for Healing the American Land* (Washington, DC: Island Press/Shearwater Books, 2004).

32   Ward, "As an activist": e-mail to the author, 2004.

6: The Millennium Arrives: November 9, 1989

38   Vaclav Havel, "It was not a bolt out of the blue": *Living in Truth: Twenty-Two Essays Published on the Occasion of the Award of the Erasmus Prize to Vaclav Havel*, ed. Jan Vladislav (London: Faber and Faber, 1987), 66.

7: The Millennium Arrives: January 1, 1994

41   Elizabeth Martínez notes, "Zapatismo rejects the idea of a vanguard leading the people . . ." in David Solnit, ed., *Globalize Liberation: How to Uproot the System and Build a Better World* (San Francisco: City Lights, 2004), from manuscript.

42   Manuel Callahan and quote in "Zapatismo Beyond Chiapas," *Globalize Liberation*, from manuscript.

44   George Orwell, "full of revolutionary sentiments": *Homage to Catalonia* (New York: Harcourt, Brace and Company, 1980), 42.

44   Fourth Declaration of the Lacandon Jungle, "A new lie is being sold to us as history," quoted in Gustavo Esteva and Madhu Suri Prakash, *Grassroots Postmodernism: Remaking the Soil of Cultures* (New York: Zed Books, 1998), 43.

8: The Millennium Arrives: November 30, 1999

48   Charles Derber writes, "The excitement of Seattle was the subliminal sense": *People Before Profit: The New Globalization in an Age of Terror, Big Money, and Economic Crisis* (New York: St. Martin's Press, 2002), 203.

49   Jose Bové, "I had the feeling that a new period": Jose Bové and François Dufour, *The World Is Not for Sale: Farmers Against Junk Food*, interviewed by Gilles Luneau, trans. Anna de Casparis (London and New York: Verso, 2001), 161.

49   Iain Boal had prophesied, "The longing for a better world...": "Up from the Bottom," in Elaine Katzenberg, ed., *First World, Ha Ha Ha!* (San Francisco: City Lights Books, 1995), 173.

50   Eddie Yuen writes, "The first of these...": in Eddie Yuen, George Katsiaficas, Daniel Burton Rose, eds., *The Battle of Seattle: The New Challenge to Capitalist Globalization* (New York: Soft Skull Press, 2001), 11.

53   George Monbiot, "At Cancun the Weak Nations Stood Up," *Guardian*, September 16, 2003.

10: The Millennium Arrives: February 15, 2003

58   The *New York Times* described popular protest as the world's other superpower. Patrick Tyler, "A New Power in the Streets," *New York Times*, February 17, 2003, www.nytimes.com/2003/02/17/world/threats-and-responses-news-analysis-a-new-power-in-the-streets.html.

59   Robert Muller exclaimed, "I'm so honored to be alive": Lynn Twist, "Waging Peace: A Story about Robert Mueller," West by Northwest.org, website, March 14, 2003.

11: Changing the Imagination of Change

61   Gandhi, "First they ignore you," in Notes from Nowhere Collective, *We Are Everywhere: The Irresistible Rise of Global Anticapitalism* (London and New York: Verso, 2003), 500.

12: On the Indirectness of Direct Action

66   Sharon Salzberg consigned the project to the "minor-good-deed category": *Faith: Trusting Your Own Deepest Experience* (New York: Riverhead Books, 2002), 139–40.

67   Borges, "You live and will die in this prison," in Jorge Luis Borges, "Infer-
     no, I, 32," *Labyrinths* (Harmondsworth, England: Penguin Books, 1970),
     273.

69   Borges, "Dante, in wonderment," ibid., 98.

69   Dante Aligheri, *Inferno*, trans. C. H. Sisson (Oxford University Press,
     1993).

69   Walter Benjamin wrote, "Every line we succeed in publishing today":
     January 11, 1940, quoted in Lloyd Spencer, online extracts from *Benja-
     min for Beginners*.

13: The Angel of Alternate History

70   Benjamin writes, "This is how one pictures the angel": Walter Benjamin,
     "Theses on the Philosophy of History," in *Illuminations: Essays and Reflec-
     tions* (New York: Schocken Books, 1969), 257.

71   Citizen Alert's biggest victory was achieved in coalition, of course, with
     various other regional and antinuclear groups.

72   Who talks about the global elimination of smallpox between 1967 and
     1977? The 2003 *Worldwatch Report* does, and that's where I was reminded
     of it.

14: Viagra for Caribou

74   Chip Ward in *Hope's Horizon*.

75   Jim Crumley, *The Last Wolf in Scotland* (Edinburgh: Birlinn Ltd, 2010).

75   Richard White, "The Natures of Nature Writing," *Raritan*, Winter 2002,
     161.

15: Getting the Hell Out of Paradise

79   Eduardo Galeano, "Utopia is on the horizon": *We Are Everywhere*, 499.

80   John Keats called the world "this vale of soul-making" in an 1819 letter to
     George and Georgiana Keats.

80   Gopal Dayaneni, "I have a soul": "War on Iraq: The Home Front," *San
     Francisco Chronicle*, March 25, 2003.

81   Walter Benjamin wrote, "The class struggle . . . is a fight for the crude and
     material things": "Theses on the Philosophy of History," in *Illuminations*,
     254.

81   Hakim Bey contrasted these moments of uprising with revolutions proper, which "lead to the expected curve," in online version of *The Temporary Autonomous Zone, Ontological Anarchy, Poetic Terrorism*, http://hermetic.com/bey/taz3.html.

16: Across the Great Divide

83   June Jordan writes, "We should take care": "Notes Toward a Black Balancing of Love and Hatred," in *Some of Us Did Not Die* (New York: Basic Civitas Books, 2003), 285.

88   Lynne Sherrod recalls, "The environmentalists and the ranchers were squared off": Phil Huffman, interview with Lynne Sherrod, *Orion Afield*, Summer 2000, 19.

88   As William DeBuys defines it, is "a departure from business as usual": William DeBuys, "Looking for the 'Radical Center,'" in *Forging a West That Works: An Invitation to the Radical Center* (Santa Fe: Quivera Coalition, 2003), 51.

89   Baldemar Velasquez says, "Number one, I don't consider anybody opposition": interview with the author, September 2003.

17: After Ideology, or Alterations in Time

91   Cornel West defined jazz "not so much as a term for a musical art form": *Race Matters* (Boston: Beacon Books, 1993), 150.

92   Charles Derber calls this the "third wave": *People Before Profit*, 205.

92   Naomi Klein remarked about global justice activists a few years ago, "When critics say the protesters lack vision": in "The Vision Thing," *The Battle of Seattle*, 314.

92   Naomi Klein, "non-hierarchical decision-making": "The Unknown Icon," Tom Hayden, ed., *The Zapatista Reader* (New York: Thunder's Mouth Press/Nation Books, 2002), 121.

93   John Jordan writes, "Our movements are trying to create": e-mail to the author, August 2003.

94   Alphonso Lingus says, "We really have to free the notion of liberation": in Mary Zournazi, *Hope: New Philosophies for Change* (New York: Routledge, 2003), 38.

94   As my brother David, a global justice organizer, sums up Holloway's position, "The notion of capturing positions of power": introduction to *Globalize Liberation: How to Uproot the System and Build a Better World* (San

Francisco: City Lights, 2003); quoting and paragraphsing John Holloway, from *Change the World without Taking Power* (London: Pluto Press, 2002).

95   Giaconda Belli writes of July 18 and 19, 1979, when the Sandinistas over-threw the Somoza regime in Nicaragua, that they were "two days that felt as if a magical": *The Country Under My Skin: A Memoir of Love and War* (New York: Alfred A. Knopf, 2003), 291.

95   Raoul Vaneigem writes, "Revolutionary moments are carnivals": quoted in *Do or Die* (Earth First! Britain's newsletter), no. 6, 1997, 4.

18: The Global Local, or Alterations in Place

96   Danny Postel, "Gray's Anatomy" (review), *The Nation*, December 22, 2003, 44.

98   Jim Dodge, "Living by Life: Some Bioregional Theory and Practice," in Lorraine Anderson, Scott Slovic, John P. O'Grady, eds., *Literature and the Environment: A Reader on Nature and Culture* (New York: Longman, 1999), 233.

100   Arundhati Roy writes of "the dismantling of the Big": quoted in Paul Hawken, "The End of Sustainability," *Bioneers Letter*, Spring 2003, 11.

19: A Dream Three Times the Size of Texas

102   Roxanne Dunbar-Ortiz, "It was the most amazing thing . . . ": conversation with the author, October 2003.

105   John Amagoalik remembers: in "Wasteland of Nobodies," in Jens Dall, Jack Hicks, and Peter Jull, eds., *Nunavut: Inuit Regain Control of Their Lands and Their Lives* (Copenhagen: International Work Group for Indigenous Affairs, 2000), 138.

20: Doubt

109   Chris Bright writes, "But the biggest obstacle to reinventing ourselves": "A History of Our Future," in *State of the World 2003: A Worldwatch Institute Report on Progress Toward a Sustainable Society* (New York: W.W. Norton, 2003), 9.

110   Subcommandante Marcos says, "History written by Power": "Flowers, Like Hope, Are Harvested," in Juana Ponce de Leon, ed., *Our Word Is Our Weapon: Selected Writings* (New York: Seven Stories Press, 2001), 173.

110   "I believe," adds Thoreau, "in the forest": Henry David Thoreau, *Walden and Other Writings* (New York: Modern Library, 1937), 613.

The Extraordinary Achievements of Ordinary People

122 "no children imprisoned": BBC News, "Young Guantanamo Afghan to Sue US," August 27, 2009, http://news.bbc.co.uk/2/hi/south_asia/8224357.stm.

122 "no unmanned drones slaughtering wedding parties": Tom Engelhardt, "Collateral Ceremonial Damage," *TomDispatch.com*, July 13, 2008, www.tomdispatch.com/post/174954.

122 "320,000 traumatic brain injuries . . . according to the RAND Corporation": RAND Corporation, press release, "One in Five Iraq and Afghanistan Veterans Suffer from PTSD or Major Depression," April 17, 2008, www.rand.org/news/press/2008/04/17.html.

Everything's Coming Together While Everything Falls Apart

126 *Guardian*, "Ursula K. Le Guin's Speech at National Book Awards: 'Books Aren't Just Commodities,'" November 20, 2014, www.theguardian.com/books/2014/nov/20/ursula-k-le-guin-national-book-awards-speech.

128 "Chevron's toxic refinery emissions": Robert Rogers, "East Bay Chevron Refinery Incident Draws Criticism, Raises Concerns about Emergency-Response Capabilities," *InsideBayArea.com*, December 19, 2014, www.insidebayarea.com/business-headlines/ci_27174056/chevron-refinery-incident-draws-criticism-raises-concerns-about?source=rss.

128 As McLaughlin put it, "We've accomplished so much...": Michael Winship, "Chevron's 'Company Town' Fights Back: An Interview with Gayle McLaughlin," *Bill Moyers & Company*, October 30, 2014, http://billmoyers.com/2014/10/30/mayor-gayle-mclaughlin.

129 "about $180 per voter": Harriet Rowan and Jimmy Tobias, "Crude Politics: Chevron Loses Expensive Election but Still Has Plenty of Power," *Richmond Confidential*, November 28, 2014, http://richmondconfidential.org/2014/11/28/crude-politics-chevron-loses-expensive-election-but-still-has-plenty-of-power.

134 "But sitting in that jail cell": Karen Mahon, "In the Battle of People vs. Pipelines, Round One Went to the People," *Observer* (Vancouver), December 6, 2014, www.vancouverobserver.com/opinion/battle-people-vs-pipelines-round-one-went-people.

About the Author

© Jude Mooney Photography

Writer, historian, and activist Rebecca Solnit is the author of eighteen books about environment, landscape, community, art, politics, hope, and memory, including *The Faraway Nearby*; *A Paradise Built in Hell: The Extraordinary Communities That Arise in Disaster*; *A Field Guide to Getting Lost*; *Wanderlust: A History of Walking*; *Men Explain Things to Me*; and *River of Shadows: Eadweard Muybridge and the Technological Wild West* (for which she received a Guggenheim, the National Book Critics Circle Award in criticism, and the Lannan Literary Award); and atlases of San Francisco and New Orleans. A product of the California public education system from kindergarten to graduate school, she is a contributing editor to *Harper's* and frequent contributor to the *Guardian* newspaper.

About Haymarket Books

Haymarket Books is a nonprofit, progressive book distributor and publisher, a project of the Center for Economic Research and Social Change. We believe that activists need to take ideas, history, and politics into the many struggles for social justice today. Learning the lessons of past victories, as well as defeats, can arm a new generation of fighters for a better world. As Karl Marx said, "The philosophers have merely interpreted the world; the point, however, is to change it."

We take inspiration and courage from our namesakes, the Haymarket Martyrs, who gave their lives fighting for a better world. Their 1886 struggle for the eight-hour day, which gave us May Day, the international workers' holiday, reminds workers around the world that ordinary people can organize and struggle for their own liberation. These struggles continue today across the globe—struggles against oppression, exploitation, hunger, and poverty.

It was August Spies, one of the Martyrs targeted for being an immigrant and an anarchist, who predicted the battles being fought to this day. "If you think that by hanging us you can stamp out the labor movement," Spies told the judge, "then hang us. Here you will tread upon a spark, but here, and there, and behind you, and in front of you, and everywhere, the flames will blaze up. It is a subterranean fire. You cannot put it out. The ground is on fire upon which you stand."

We could not succeed in our publishing efforts without the generous financial support of our readers. Many people contribute to our project through the Haymarket Sustainers program, where donors receive free books in return for their monetary support. If you would like to be a part of this program, please contact us at info@haymarketbooks.org. Shop our full catalog online at www.haymarketbooks.org.

Also available
from Haymarket Books

Capitalism: A Ghost Story
Arundhati Roy

The End of Imagination
Arundhati Roy

Exoneree Diaries: The Fight for Innocence, Independence, and Identity
Alison Flowers

Failure to Quit: Reflections of an Optimistic Historian
Howard Zinn

*Freedom Is a Constant Struggle: Ferguson, Palestine,
and the Foundations of a Movement*
**Angela Y. Davis, edited by Frank Barat,
foreword by Dr. Cornel West**

Men Explain Things to Me
Rebecca Solnit

Live Working or Die Fighting: How the Working Class Went Global
Paul Mason

On History: Tariq Ali and Oliver Stone in Conversation
Oliver Stone and Tariq Ali

On Palestine
Noam Chomsky and Ilan Pappé, edited by Frank Barat

The Speech: The Story Behind Dr. Martin Luther King Jr.'s Dream
Gary Younge